Collins

Learn to Pai

Landscapes in Oils

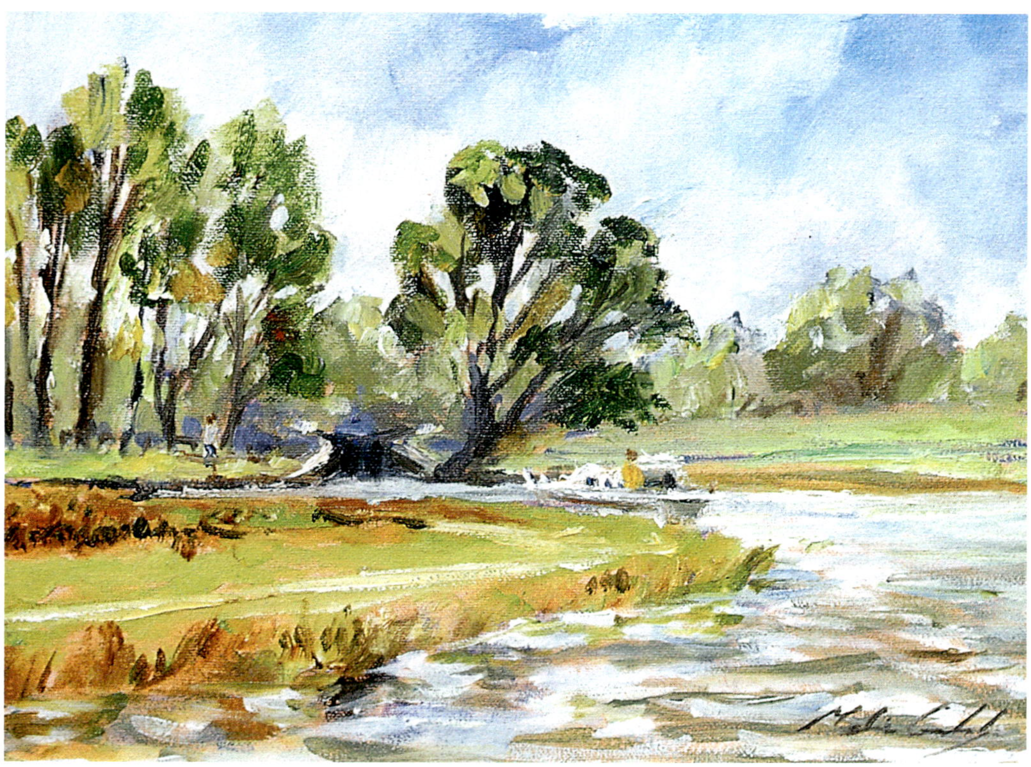

Melanie Cambridge

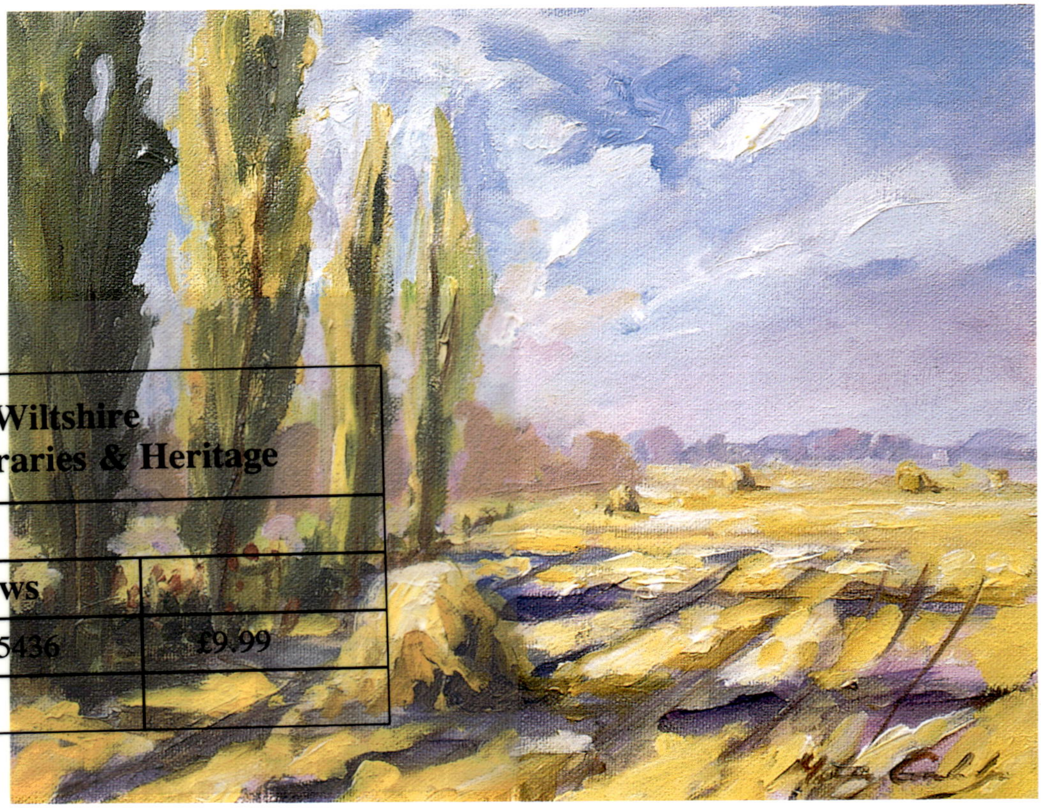

First published in 2004 by
Collins, an imprint of
HarperCollins*Publishers*
77-85 Fulham Palace Road
Hammersmith, London W6 8JB

The Collins website address is www.collins.co.uk

05 07 09 08 06 04
2 4 6 8 7 5 3 1

A catalogue record for this book is available from the British Library.

Editor: Geraldine Christy
Designer: Penny Dawes
Photographer: Laura Knox

ISBN 0 00 717034 3

Colour reproduction by Colourscan, Singapore
Printed and bound by Printing Express Ltd, Hong Kong

Previous page: **Cruising Along** 25 x 30 cm (10 x 12 in)
This page: **Late Summer Shadows** 20 x 25 cm (8 x 10 in)
Opposite: **Sunday Afternoon, Richmond** 46 x 59 cm (18 x 22 in)

Contents

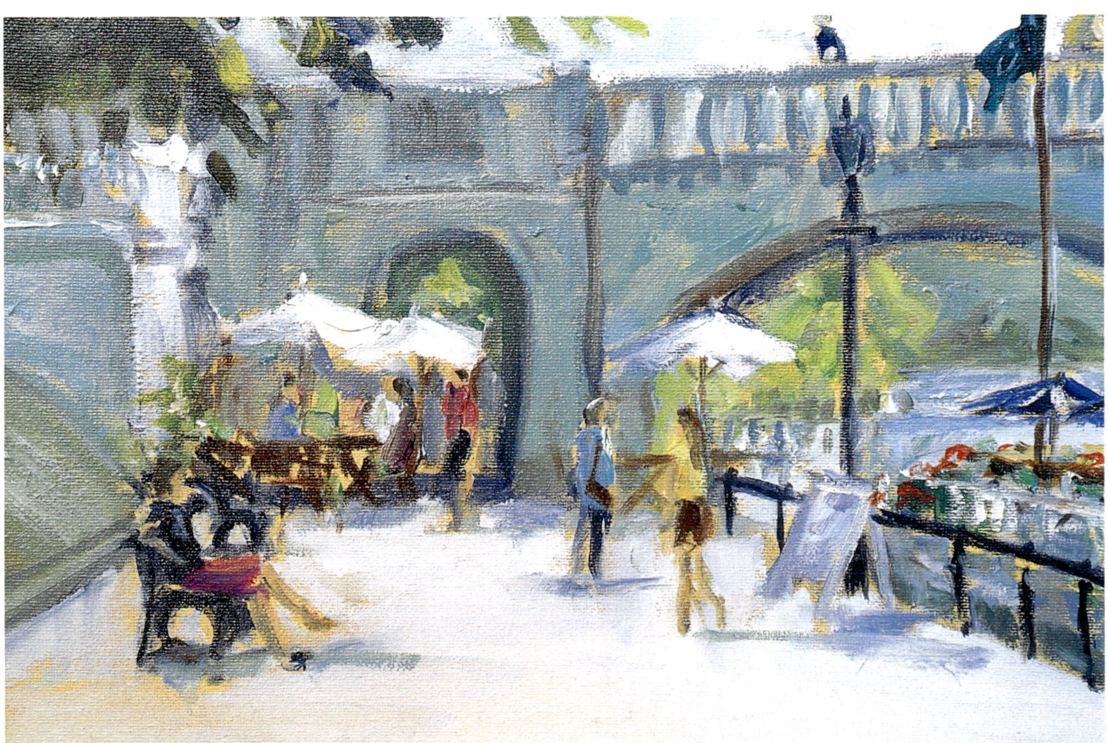

Portrait of an Artist

Melanie Cambridge was born and grew up in Cheshire, but now lives in Surrey where she paints and writes. She has always enjoyed painting the landscape and works outdoors whenever possible (even in winter). Oils have been her first-choice medium for painting ever since she was a child – the quality of the paint, the varying textures, and the ability to change and rework any part of the painting at any stage, are just some of the reasons she prefers oils to any other medium.

Melanie has a lifelong interest in art and painted in oils from a relatively early age. However, she did not achieve artistic success while at school as the emphasis at the time was on abstract art rather than the more traditional styles of painting that interested her. Instead of going to art school she decided to concentrate on earning a living

▼ Melanie Cambridge painting in her studio.

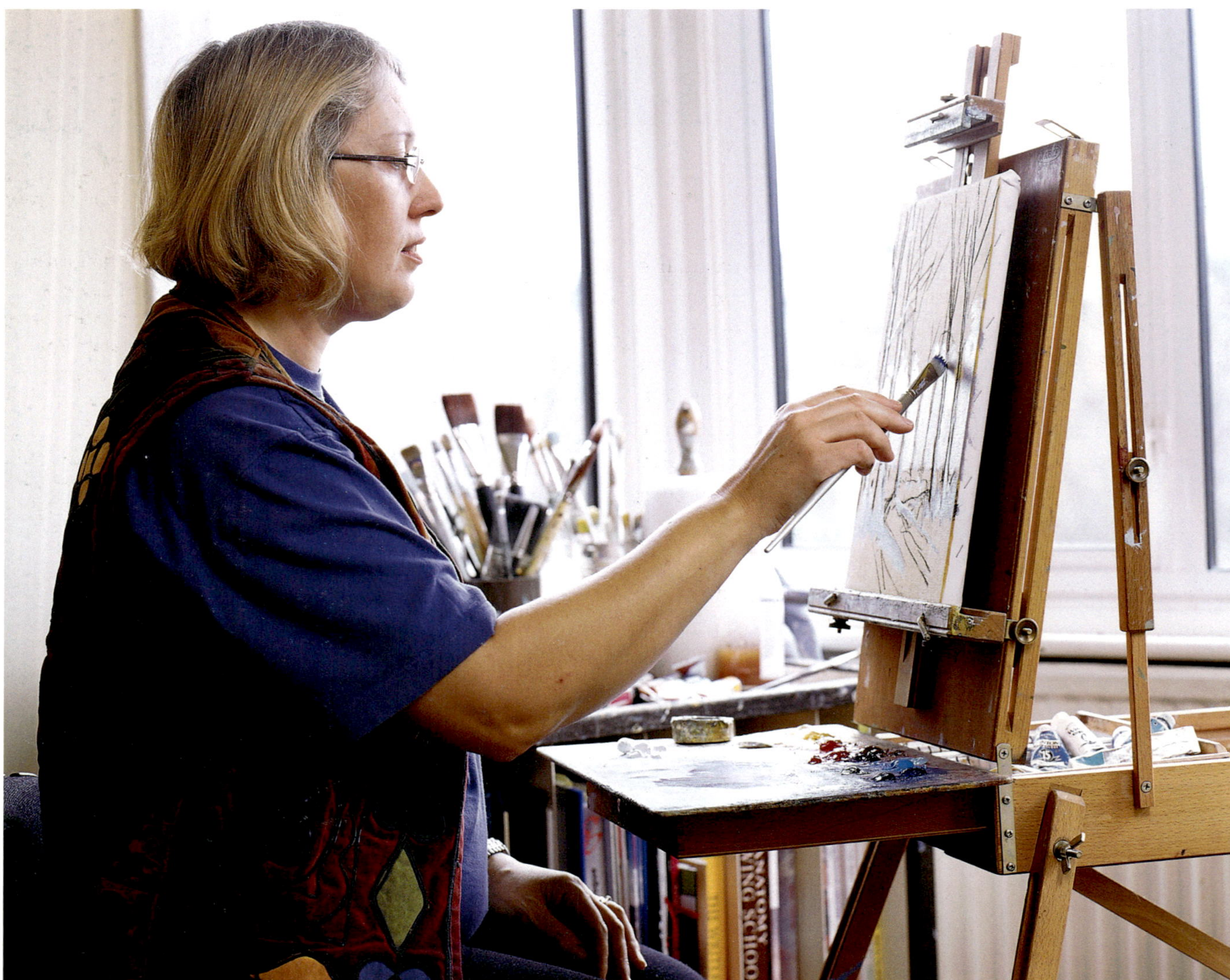

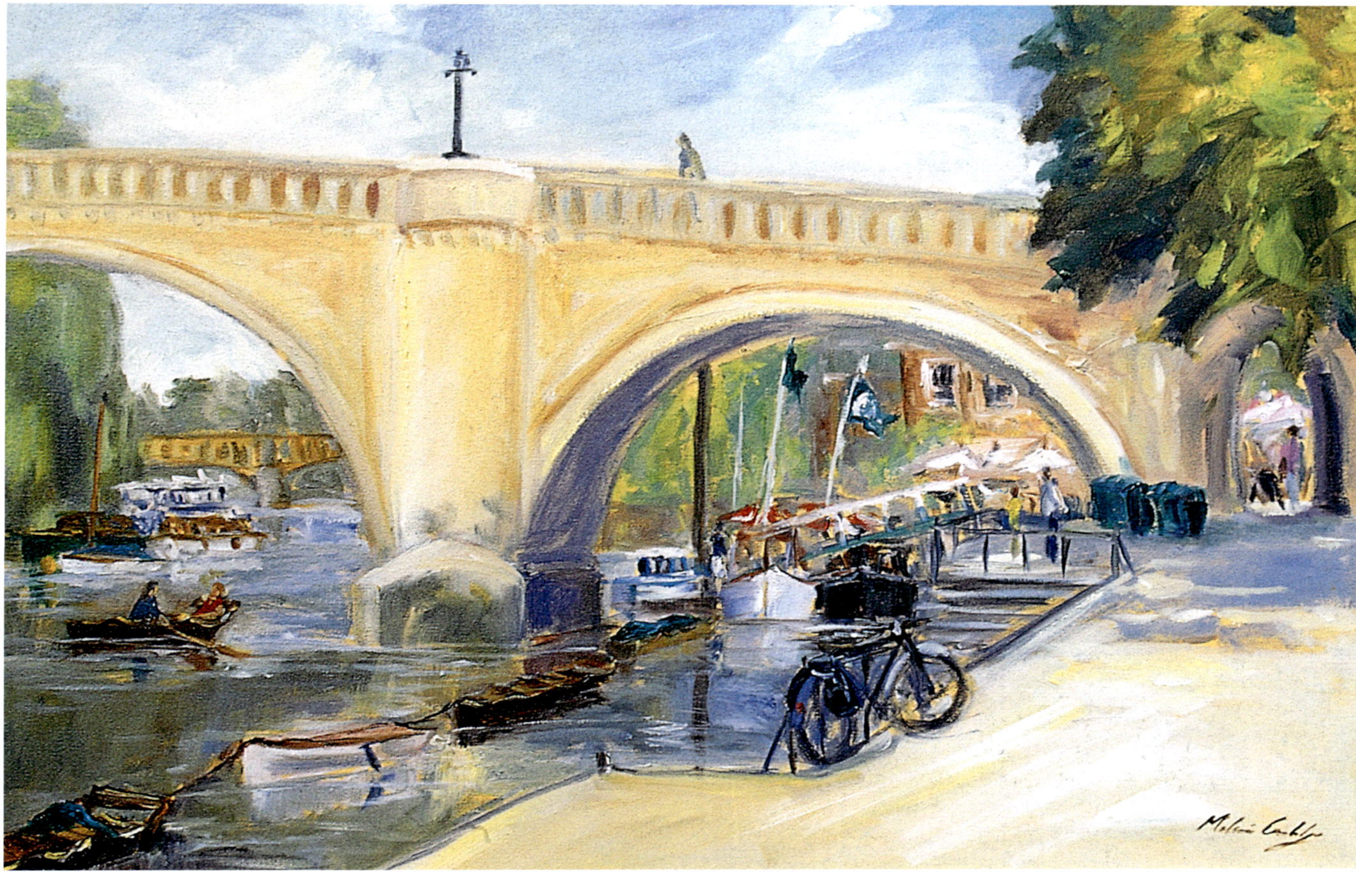

in the financial world instead. This was a disappointment at the time, but she continued to paint and develop her own style. She finally gave up her administrative position to concentrate on painting full time in the mid 1990s after two successful exhibitions in London.

Over the years the influences on Melanie's work have changed and, while she still travels abroad to paint, being particularly attracted to the light of the Mediterranean and southern France, she is finding more and more interest in the area around her home. Melanie recently joined the Guild of Waterway Artists and now finds herself tackling a new range of subjects along the Thames and River Wey as well as canals around the country.

Keen to encourage art in others, Melanie runs various painting courses in south-east England, and is a frequent visitor to art societies around the country, demonstrating and teaching mainly oils. She is also a regular contributor to *Artists & Illustrators* magazine. Her previous books, *Success with Oils* and *You Can Paint Acrylics* (both published by Collins), have been well received, as has her oils instruction video of the same title.

Melanie believes in working from life whenever possible. For a landscape painter this can sometimes result in painting outdoors in snow and rain as well as on sunny days! Oil paints might seem cumbersome when compared to other mediums, but she feels the immediacy and flexibility of working in oils makes a little extra time spent organizing the equipment a small price to pay.

Melanie's approach to teaching is to emphasize that relatively few items of equipment are essential for the landscape painter in oils. With a palette of just ten colours she encourages the beginner to create wonderful paintings that capture the many moods of the landscape.

▲ **Sunday Afternoon, Richmond Bridge**
41 x 61 cm (16 x 24 in)
This was painted on location on a hot summer's day. Fortunately, the owner of the bicycle did not return until after the work was complete.

Painting Landscapes in Oils

For many artists, painting the landscape out in the open is one of the most enjoyable, exciting and sometimes exasperating experiences there is! For me, there is nothing quite as wonderful as working in the open air, trying to capture the scene in front of me before the light changes and the whole view takes on a different aspect. If you are new to landscape painting, though, please do not feel that you must head up to the hills or out into the wildest country. Your garden or the local park can offer plenty of interesting subject matter for a landscape. In fact, it is often better to start by painting places that are familiar to you, where you are more likely to feel at home and relaxed.

Oil paints are ideal for landscape subjects. The colours have a wonderful buttery texture and can be used in a direct manner, so you can establish the main structure of your painting quickly and easily. Oil paints are also extremely flexible. If you make a mistake, simply wipe it out and carry on. Because oils take a few days to dry, you can still change your mind the next morning. This makes the medium ideal for beginners, helping to take away the belief that every brushstroke on the canvas has to be right first time.

If you change your mind after several days, wait until the paint is fully dry before overpainting. Otherwise there is a risk that the top layer will crack.

▼ Painting the Poppies
30 x 51 cm (12 x 20 in)
I came across this mass of vibrant poppies while walking near my home. Not having any paints with me, I made a quick sketch and dashed back to the studio to paint the picture immediately while the colours were still fresh in my mind.

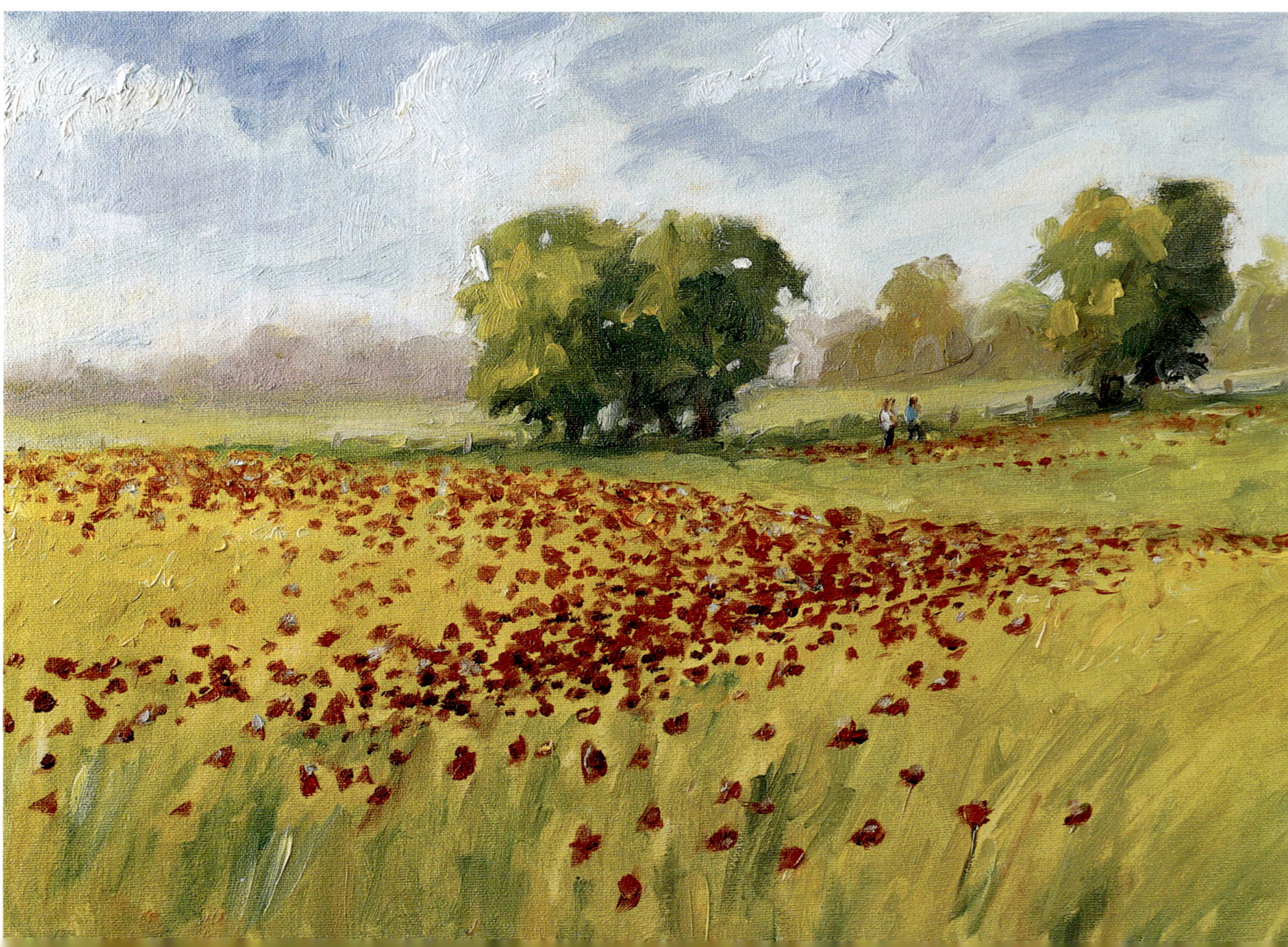

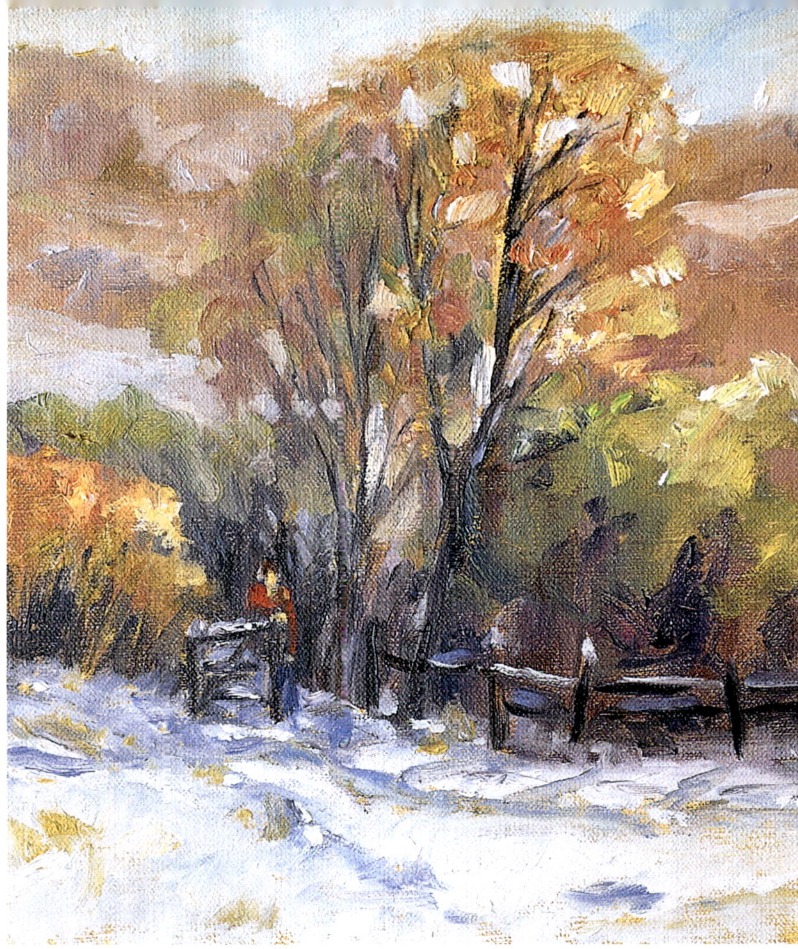

▶ **Winter Walk, North Downs**
30 x 25 cm (12 x 10 in)
This was painted on location near my home after the first snowfall of the winter. The figure walking up the path was an added bonus.

Using sketchbooks

Of course it is not always possible to go outside to paint landscapes, nor do all artists wish to do so. Some will work mainly from photographs, sketches or even their imagination. For those times when you do not have your paintbox with you, I suggest that you carry a sketchbook – mine is very small, just 15 x 10 cm (6 x 4 in), and easily fits into a jacket pocket or a handbag. Rather than a pencil, I prefer to use a cartridge drawing pen and keep several spare cartridges in my purse, so I always have them at hand. By carrying a sketchbook all the time, you will be ready to make quick sketches of anything that catches your eye. Not only does this help you build up information for future paintings, but it will also help you to develop your 'eye' as an artist.

How this book can help

Before you take the plunge into landscapes it is important to spend some time learning the basic techniques of oil painting. This book will guide you through the process and help you to discover the joy of working in oils and also to develop your own technical skills in handling oil paint.

Oils are perhaps the most exciting of all the painting media. They can be used entirely wet-in-wet, which can be an exhilarating way to paint. Once fully dry, they can be over-painted, either with opaque paint to block out and change some areas of the painting, or by applying glazes or scumbling to add depth and subtlety to your landscapes. So, as well as looking at the obvious areas of mixing colours and basic techniques for applying paint to canvas, I have tried to show you how to manipulate oils for a wide range of effects. This knowledge of how to handle oil paint will help you to realize your own potential as an artist and learn how to express yourself in the way that suits you best.

▼ A quick ink sketch made while being driven through the Swiss Alps.

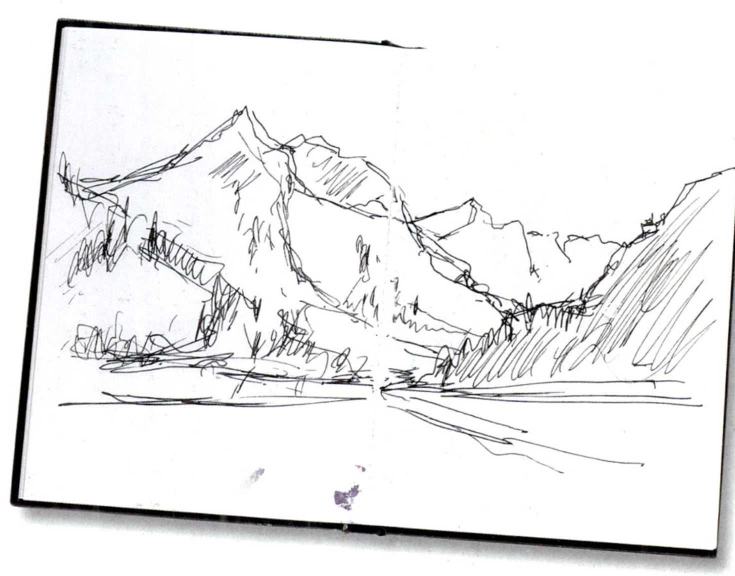

Materials and Equipment

When you first start to paint with oils, it is easy to find yourself buying lots of equipment you do not really need. So, to help you avoid this, I suggest that you start with a basic range of ten colours, a few brushes and a bottle of alkyd gel medium.

Colours

Oil paints come in tubes of various sizes, and 37 ml is a good size to begin with. I would recommend having a larger tube of white (say 120 ml) – you will need to add white for mixing paler colours and will tend to use more of this than your other colours. Paints are available in both artists' quality and less expensive student-quality grades. I have used student-quality paints for the demonstrations in this book.

To simplify matters, start with just a few tubes and learn to mix these colours first. You can easily add others as your confidence and ability increases. For a starter palette for landscapes I recommend: Lemon Yellow, Yellow Ochre, Naples Yellow, Vermilion, Venetian Red, Cobalt Violet, Rose Madder, Coeruleum, French Ultramarine, Cobalt Blue and Titanium White.

As you will see, there is no ready-mixed green in this basic landscape palette. I suggest you try first to mix your green shades using the different yellows and blues in your selection. This will give you a better understanding of colour use.

Brushes and surfaces

Traditionally, oil brushes were made of hog hair. However, there are now several ranges of nylon brushes on the market for oils. They are a little softer than hog hair, but still have enough 'spring' for oil painting.

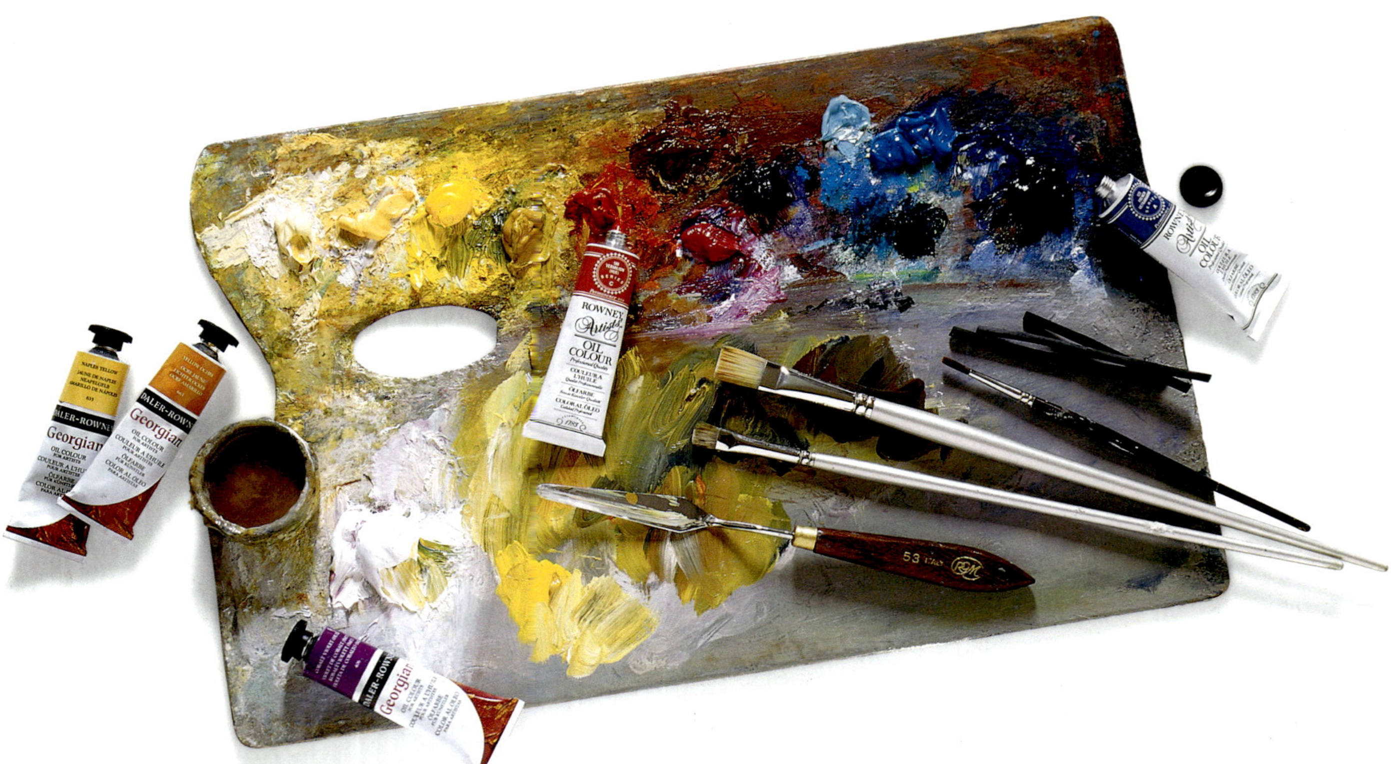

▼ My working palette loaded with colour. Just a few brushes, a palette knife and a basic selection of tubes of paint are all that you need to make a start.

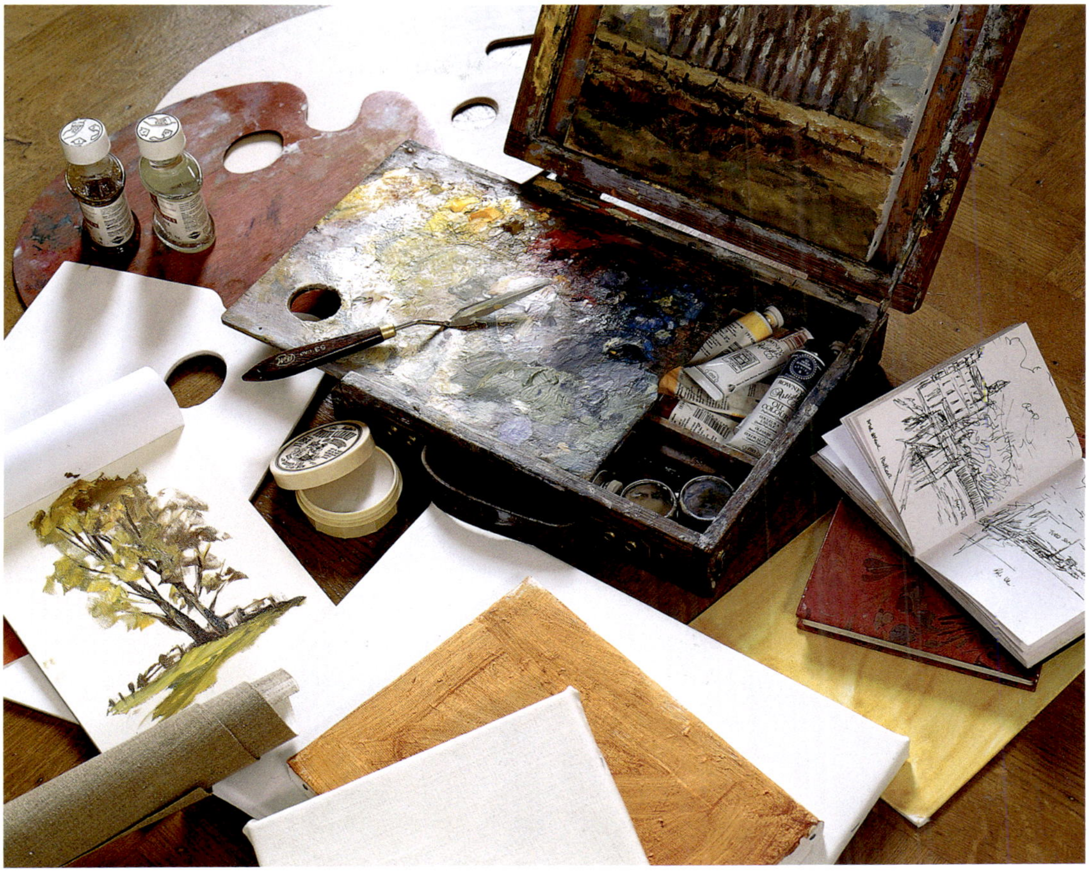

◀ A pochade box will hold a small panel as well as your painting materials. Choose a variety of sketchbooks, textured pads and canvas boards for outdoor work.

I recommend you start with just two or three brushes from the following sizes: a 25 mm (1 in) short flat bright, a 12 mm (½ in) short flat bright, a 6 mm (¼ in) short flat bright; plus a No. 4 round brush.

The traditional painting surface for oils is primed and stretched canvas. This is wonderful to paint on, but various less costly alternatives are perfectly acceptable. A pad of oil-sketching paper makes a good investment; this is specially coated paper with a textured surface similar to canvas.

Mediums

There are many mediums on the market for use with oil paints, including the traditional turpentine and linseed oil. For simplicity, I suggest you use just one – alkyd gel medium. This has virtually no odour, is safe to use indoors without having to open a window, and also helps to speed up the drying time. Since this medium is a gel rather than a liquid, the painting surface remains sticky rather than slippery, making it easier to work another layer of wet paint without muddying lower layers. Gel medium also helps you to paint thin glazes.

Oil brushes need to be properly cleaned at the end of each painting session, so you will need a general-purpose brush cleaner such as white spirit or brush-cleaning fluid.

Other materials

It is helpful to have an easel or some sort of support that enables you to have your painting surface fairly upright as you work. A wooden box easel or a smaller pochade box will hold your paints, brushes and palette, as well as a wet oil painting. Use a palette knife for mixing your colours.

While painting, you will need plenty of rags or kitchen paper for wiping your brushes to remove most of the excess paint before changing colours.

Mixing Colours

Time spent learning to mix colours is never time wasted. While you may be keen to get on with making a painting, please do not be tempted to skip over the following pages on colour. Even as you become more experienced as an artist, do try to put aside just a few moments at the beginning of each painting session to experiment with some of the colours on your palette. This will pay tremendous dividends as you develop as an artist, helping to build your confidence as well as your knowledge and ability to control colour.

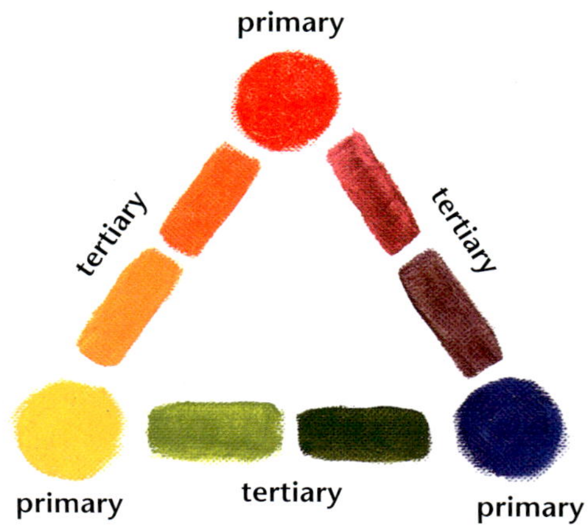

◀ This colour triangle shows the three primaries (circle shapes) linked by the tertiary colours produced when they are mixed together.

Using primaries

The three primary colours – red, yellow and blue – are familiar to most people from painting lessons at school. When two primaries are mixed together they give the three secondary colours of orange, green and purple. Mixing a primary with a related secondary produces a tertiary colour that shows the stronger influence made by the dominant primary shade.

In theory it should be possible to mix every colour you need from three primaries, but in practice this is difficult to achieve. This is because colour theory is based on the light spectrum. Manufactured paints, however, tend to have a slight bias towards another colour and so do not behave as pure colour when they are mixed together.

► My palette has a warm and a cool version of most colours.

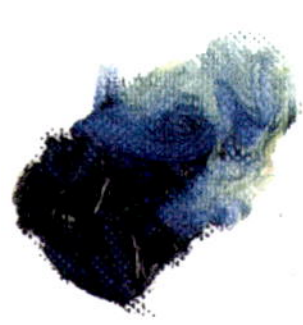

Cobalt Blue
A strong cool blue, slightly biased towards yellow.

Cobalt Violet
A strong purple with a bias towards blue.

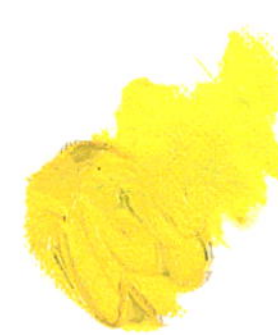

Lemon Yellow
A cold yellow with a bias towards green; useful for mixing bright spring greens.

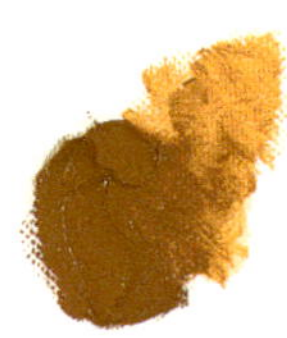

Yellow Ochre
A warm earth yellow.

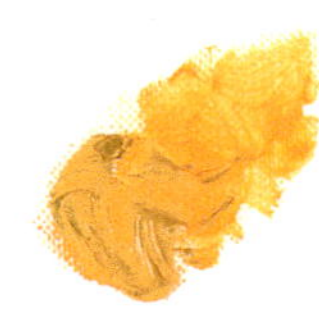

Naples Yellow
A warm cream shade; useful for mixing with Cobalt Violet for greys.

Titanium White
A cold white that has excellent coverage and mixes well for tints.

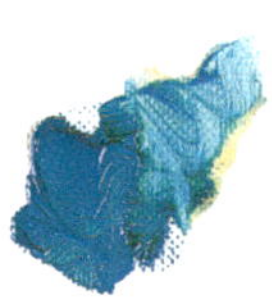

Coeruleum
A cool turquoise blue, very similar to pure primary blue.

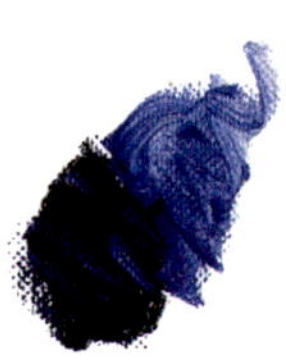

French Ultramarine
A deep blue with a bias towards red.

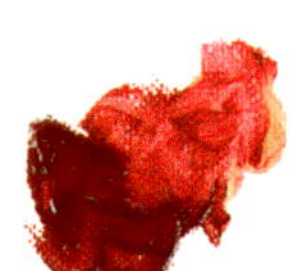

Rose Madder
A cool pink colour.

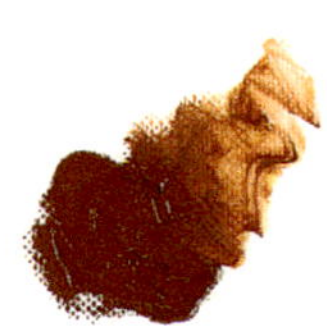

Venetian Red
A warm reddish brown; mixed with French Ultramarine makes dark tones.

Vermilion
A pure warm red; excellent for mixing orange shades or warm greys.

Understanding the colour bias and using it to your advantage is one of the keys to successful colour mixing.

It is a good idea to look at your basic palette of colours carefully and consider the individual characteristics of each one.

Warm and cool colours

I have described many of the colours of my basic palette as being either 'warm' or 'cool'. In general, warm colours are those with a red or orange bias, while cool colours are those with a green or blue bias. You can use this awareness of warm and cool colours in your work to help enhance the effect of depth and distance in your landscapes. Warm colours appear to come forward in a painting and thus are most effective in the foreground, while cool colours seem further away, so may be used towards the horizon.

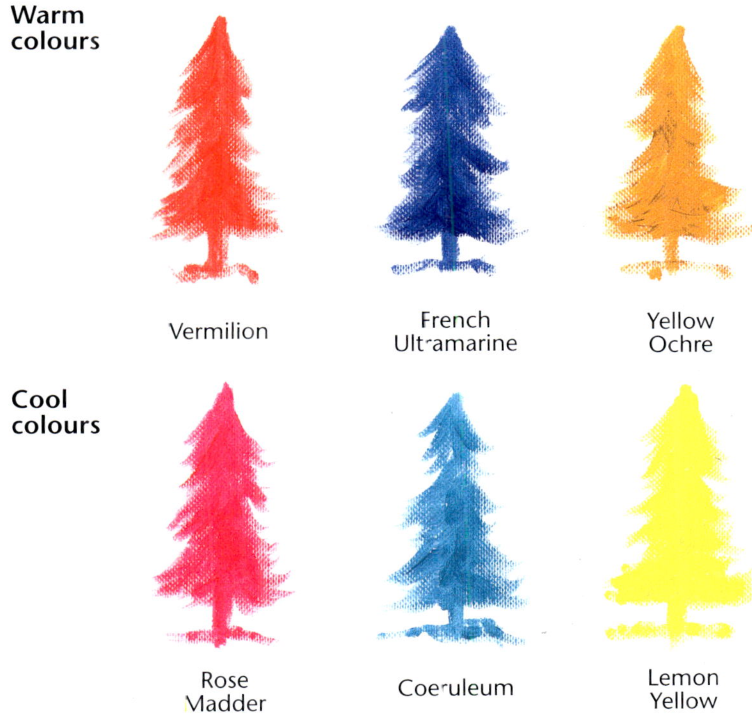

The difference between objects near to and further away may not always be very obvious, particularly when the weather is clear and sunny. However, by using your understanding of warm and cool colours to select a cooler, bluer shade of green for trees in the distance, they will automatically appear 'right' in your finished painting.

Think of your landscape as a piece of music. For objects in the far distance, the music is very quiet and soft, so make your distant colours soft, blue and cool. As objects come forward in the painting, so their colours generally appear warmer and with stronger contrasts, just as music is louder and with greater contrast when its source is nearer to your ear.

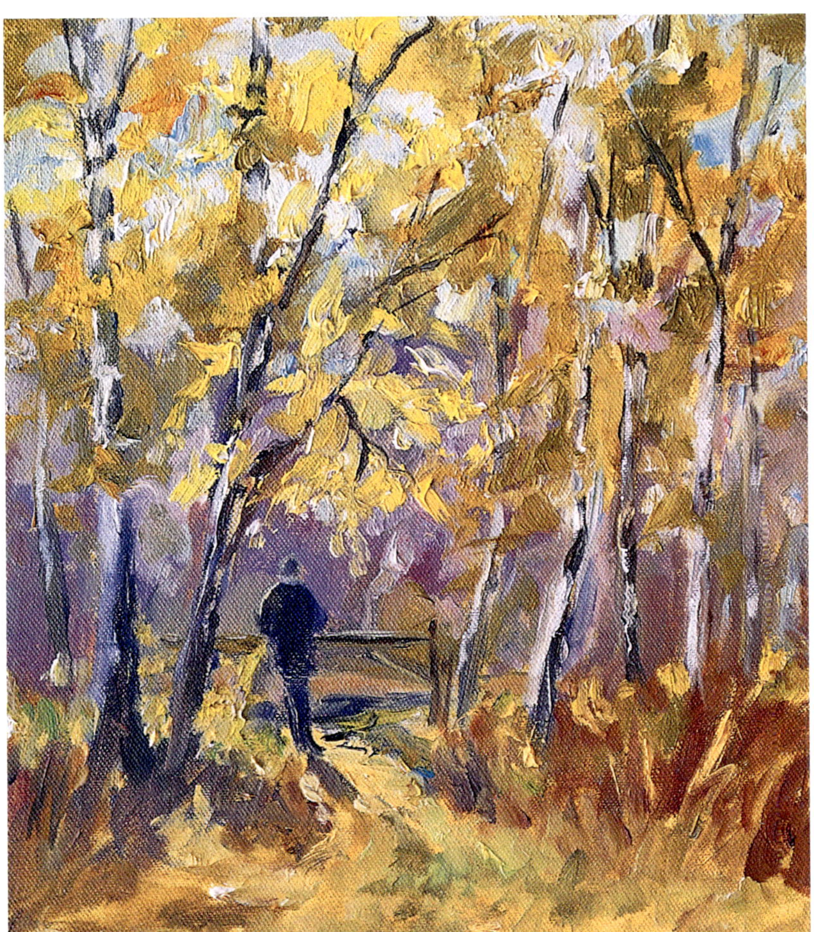

◀ **Autumn Colours, Wisley**
30 x 25 cm (12 x 10 in)
In this woodland scene I have used much cooler shades for the deeper part of the wood, helping it recede into the distance, against the warm yellows and oranges of the autumn foliage on the foreground trees.

Complementary colours

The three primary colours, with their three secondary mixes in between, are often shown as a colour circle or wheel. Colours opposite each other on the wheel are termed complementary, a primary being opposite the secondary made from the other two primary colours. This gives paired complementaries of red and green, blue and orange, and yellow and purple.

Colours for shadows

A useful aid in mixing colours is to use complementary colours to create darker shades. In each case, by adding a little of the colour that is complementary to the initial colour you can mix a darker 'shadow' version of it.

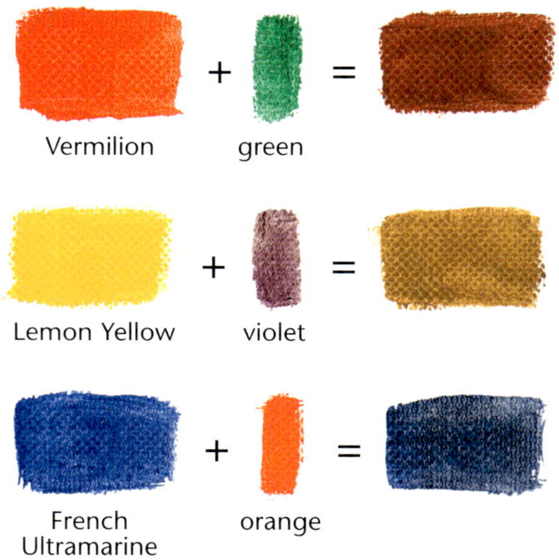

◀ Creating 'shadow' colours by adding the complementary.

Mixing black

I find black a very insistent colour for oil painting and one that can easily dominate colour mixes, so I prefer to avoid it. For the beginner it can be tempting simply to mix a little black into colours for darker shades. While doing so will produce darker colours, these tend to be dull and lifeless. It is far preferable to mix darker tones by adding a little of the appropriate complementary colour.

For those times when you need a really dark shade (almost black) try mixing French Ultramarine with a little Venetian Red. This gives a much richer tone, which can be either a dark brown (if you have more Venetian Red in the mix) or a wonderful blue-black shade (if you start with French Ultramarine and add only a very little Venetian Red).

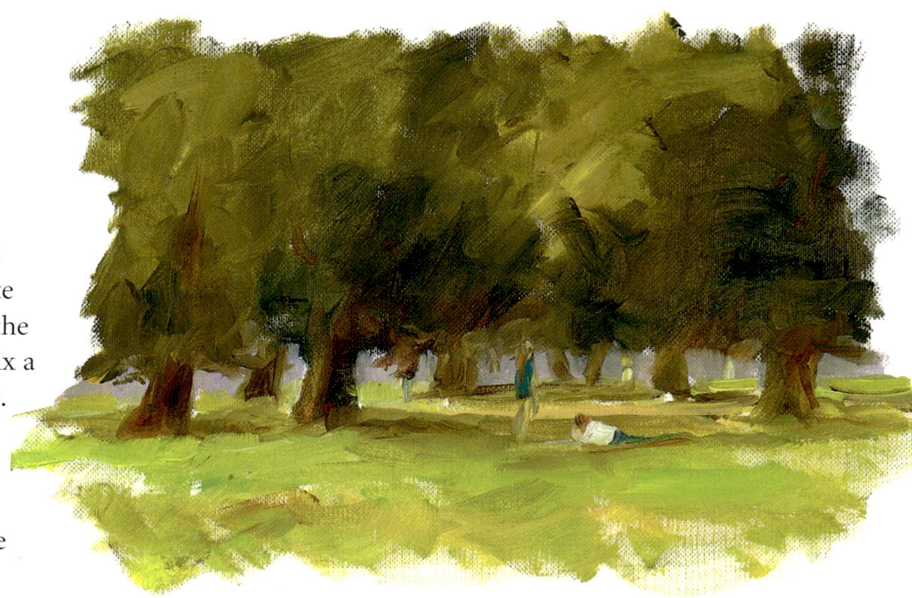

▲ In this study of Green Park, London, the initial tree green was mixed from Yellow Ochre and French Ultramarine, with Lemon Yellow and Coeruleum for the parkland beneath. All of the shadows in the trees and on the grass were mixed by adding a little complementary colour, Venetian Red, to the original green.

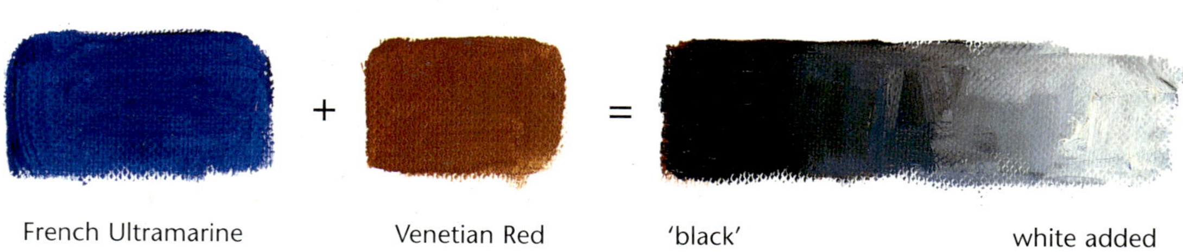

◀ See how many different dark shades can be created using French Ultramarine and Venetian Red. For grey, add a little white to the mix.

Mixing greens

Green is a key colour for any landscape painter, so it is important to understand how to mix different shades. As you can see from the examples here, it is possible to mix many different shades using only two yellows and two blues. In each case start with the predominant colour and add a little of the second colour slowly to reach the desired shade. If you are mixing a yellow-green colour, it makes sense to start with yellow and then add a little blue rather than the other way round. Not only is it easier to mix the shade you wish, but you will use much less paint. You can see from the mixes here just how much more of the predominant colour you need compared to the second colour. I have also added white to each green shade to give a paler version.

Follow my examples first, and then experiment with some mixes of your own. You may find it helpful to keep examples of green mixes to refer back to in order to mix a specific colour in the future. Write the names alongside each colour for an accurate record.

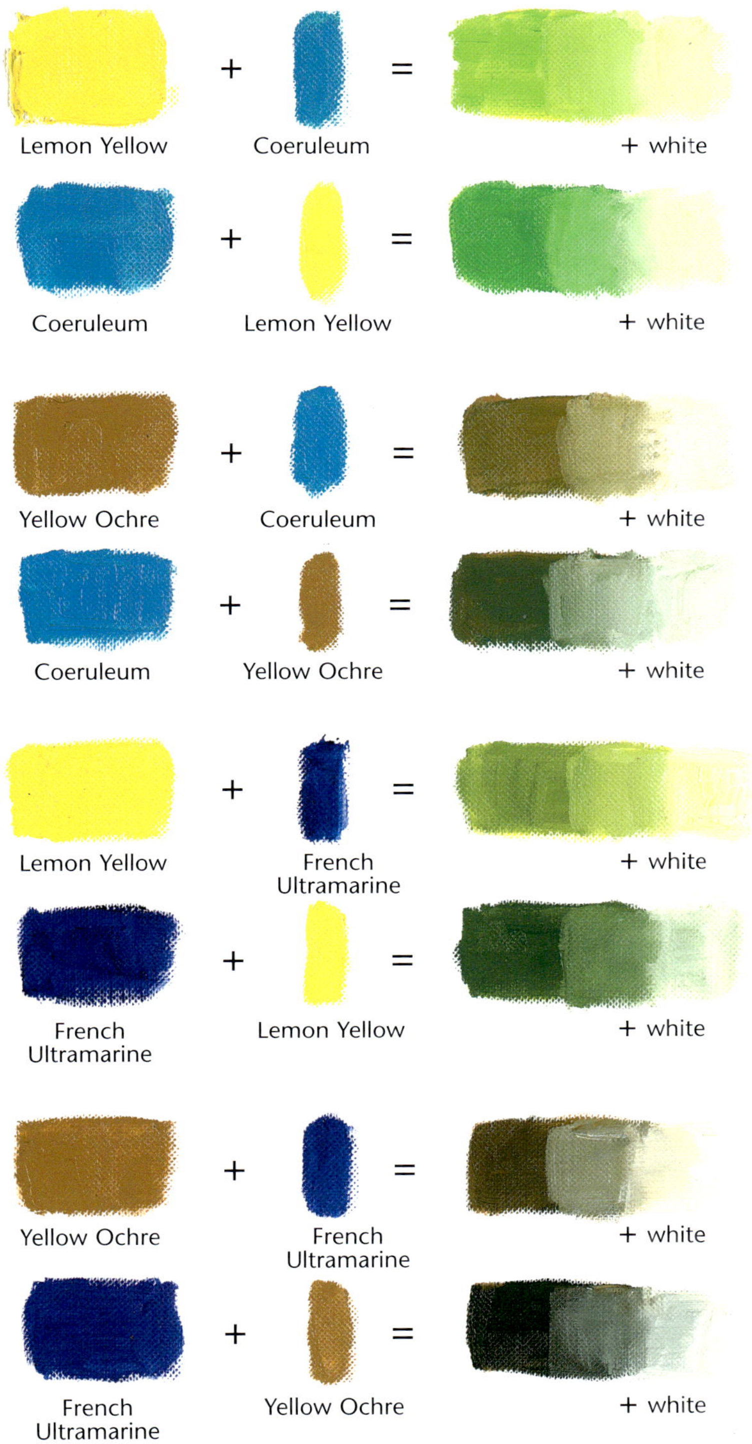

◀ Use yellows and blues in different proportions to mix many greens.

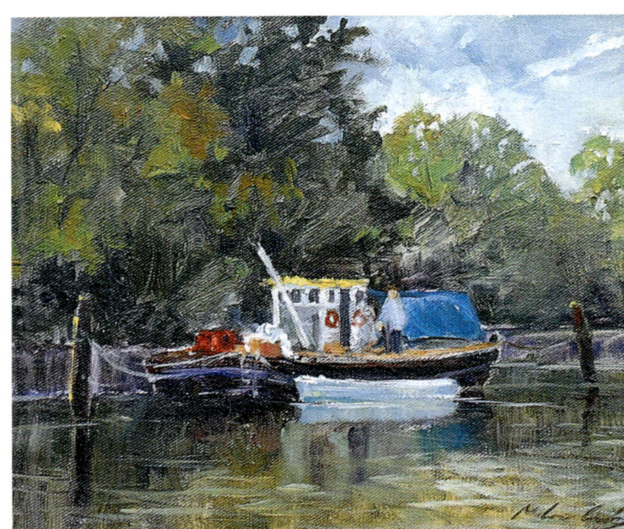

▶ **Quiet Mooring, River Thames**
25 x 30 cm (10 x 12 in)
The subtle changes of tone and colour of the trees on the riverbank from a warm green to a softer, cooler blue-green help to create a feeling of recession.

Oil Techniques

For oil painting, more than most other media, the variety of marks you can produce with a single brush is perhaps the key to a pleasing and successful picture.

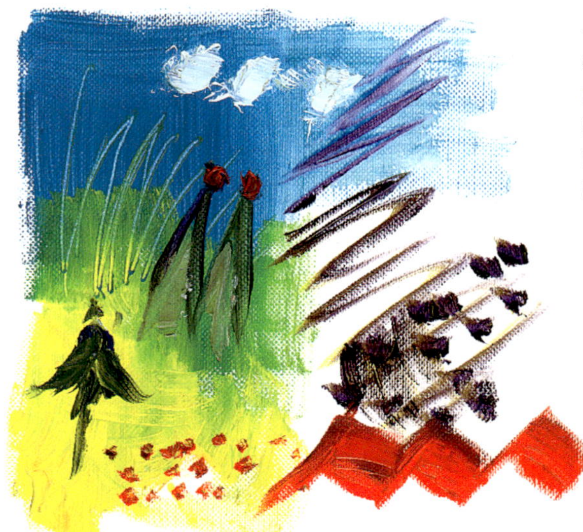

◀ Brushstroke doodles should not make any sense. Simply enjoy making as many marks as you can.

The power of the brush

A single brushstroke can capture so much in oil painting, so make friends with your brush. Start just by doodling. Use the 12mm (½ in) flat brush and aim to make as many different marks and textures as you can. Vary the amount of paint; thin it with plenty of medium; use it thickly from the tube; even try scratching into the surface with the wrong end of the brush. Also vary the direction of your brushstrokes.

These are just a few suggestions; the more confident you become in handling both your brush and paint, the faster you will develop your own style of painting.

Wet techniques

Oil paint dries slowly over three or four days, so all the initial work will involve working one wet layer on top of existing wet paint – that is, working 'wet-in-wet'. This makes it easy to change your mind as you go along, wiping off any mistakes and repainting areas before they dry. While this is a wonderfully free and exciting way to paint, it takes a little practice until you become confident in handling the paint texture and colour mixes.

Wet-in-wet

Simple exercises will help to improve your brush control and ability to move paint around the canvas. Start by blocking in a layer of a dark colour and then try adding patches of lighter colours on top. You will need to work very delicately when adding the lighter colours. Hold the brush halfway along the handle, load it with plenty of colour and then use light pressure to carefully place the second colour onto the underlying wet dark paint. The action is almost as if you were spreading butter.

▼ For this wet-in-wet exercise I painted the red dinghy and blue ripples carefully on top of a thin wet layer of Yellow Ochre.

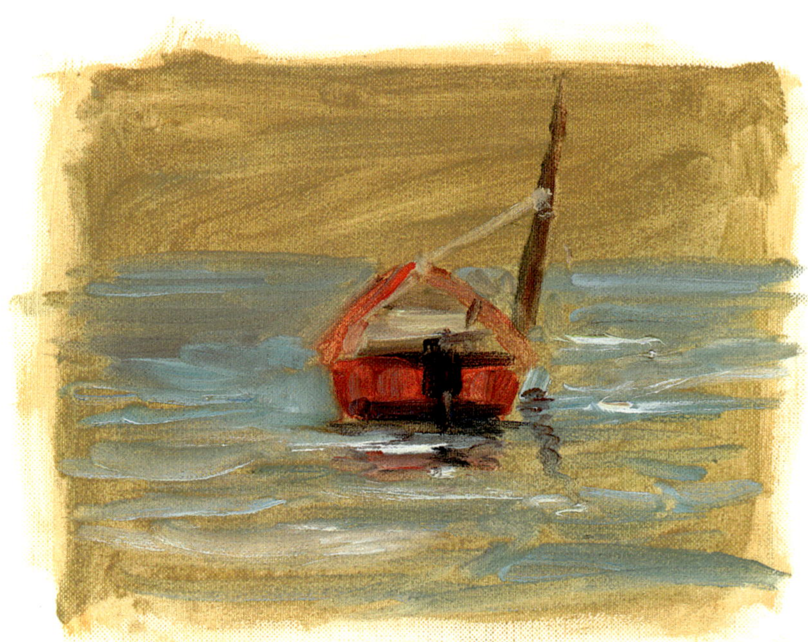

Quality of edge

As well as varying your brushstrokes the quality of edge (where one colour meets another) is an important feature in oil painting. Whether the edge of one area, object or patch of colour is sharp and clean against another colour, or slightly blurred or almost lost where colours have been blended together, is a key technique.

A sharp or hard edge between two objects creates a clear line of definition, useful for placing one object behind another. A soft edge can add a little mystery, blending misty trees towards the horizon or softening the edge of a cloud.

Where the edge of one feature is blurred against another it is sometimes referred to as a 'lost' edge. Alternatively, hard edges that show clear contrast of tone or colour may be called 'found'.

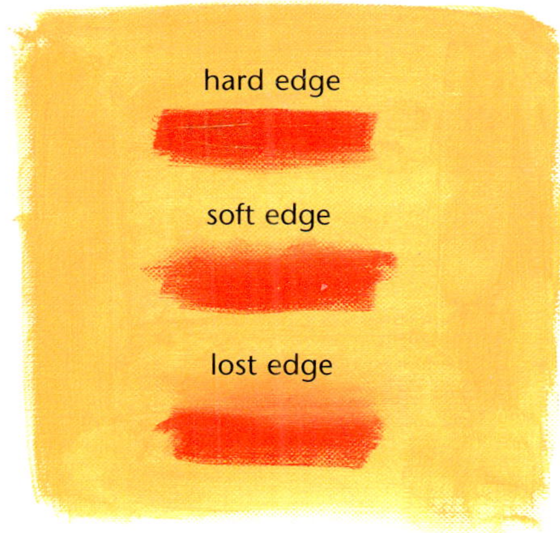

◄ An important feature of oil painting is the quality of the edge in creating illusion and mood.

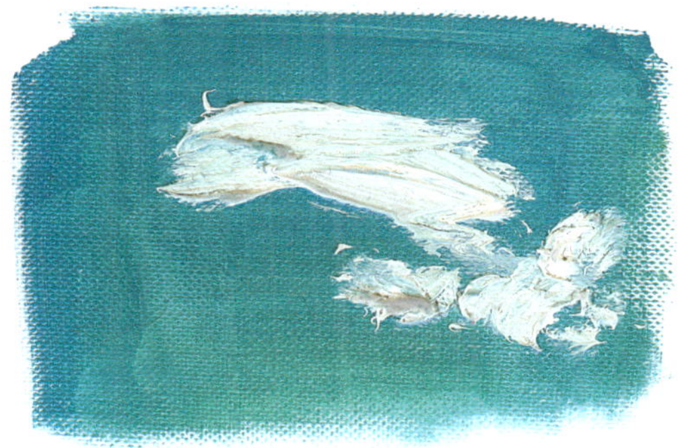

◄ Thick paint areas such as this are known as impasto.

Thin darks to thicker lights

For oil painting it is usual to start with the darkest colours and work towards the lightest. This is possible because oil paints are generally opaque, so a light colour will cover a darker one. Aim to start with thinner applications of colour for the dark areas and gradually work towards thicker paint for the lighter areas, reserving your heaviest paint texture for the highlights.

Impasto

The application of very thick paint is known as 'impasto'. This technique can be very effective, but use it sparingly. Keep it for areas such as where the sun catches the light edge of a cloud or the distant glint of light on water, ideally alongside the strongest darks where it can have the greatest impact.

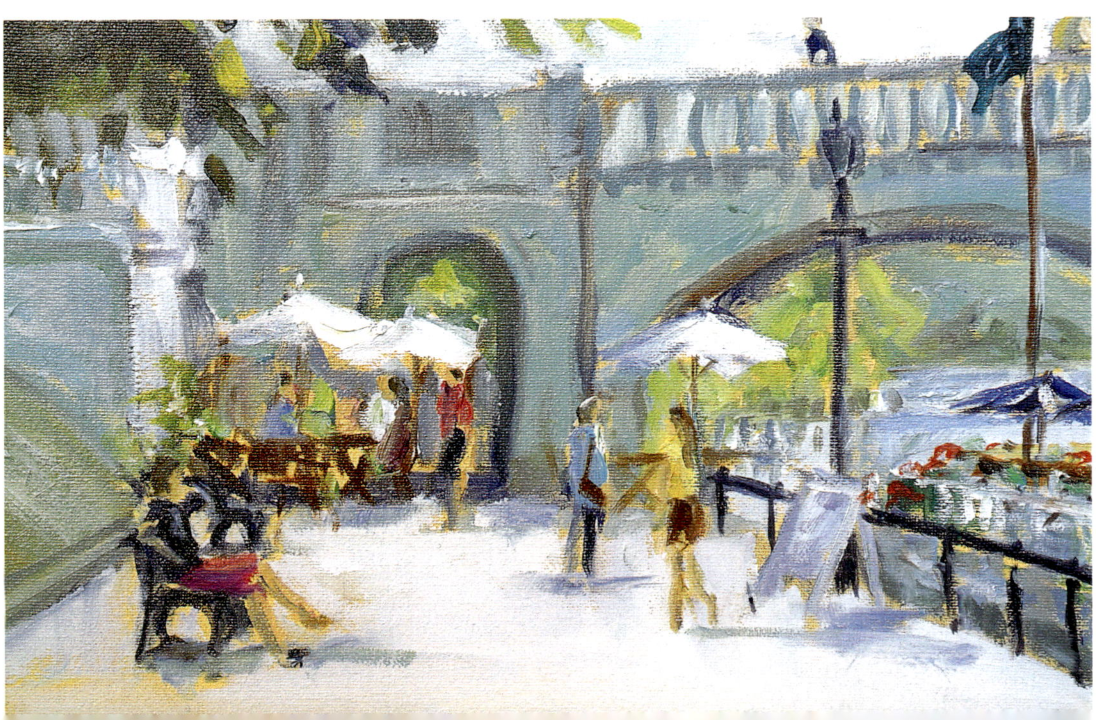

◄ **Sunday Afternoon, Richmond**
46 x 59 cm (18 x 22 in)
I have used the heaviest impasto only for the white umbrellas of the café, helping them stand out against the thinly painted shadows on the bridge.

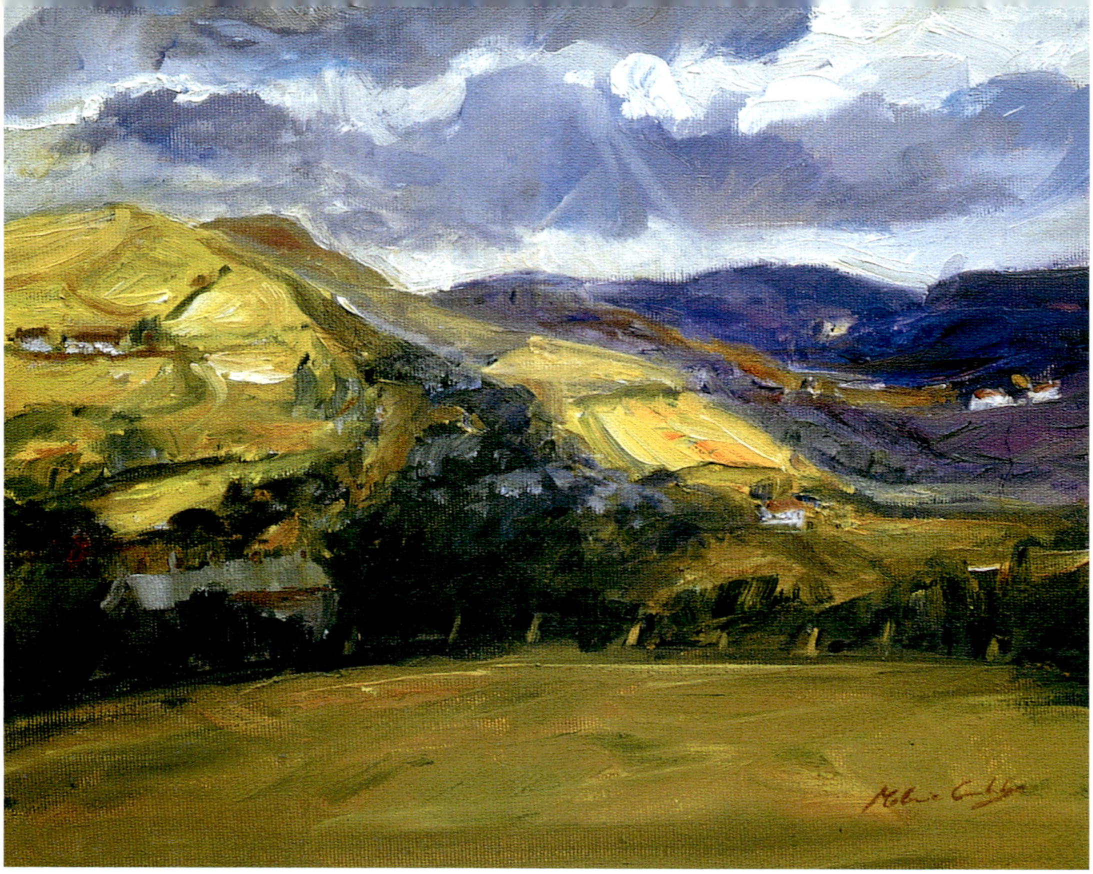

◀ Sunlight and Shadows over the High Peak
25 x 30 cm (10 x 12 in)
A thin glaze of French Ultramarine was painted over the foreground to darken it, emphasizing the sunlight on the left-hand hillside.

Dry techniques

The techniques described so far are generally used when working wet-in-wet. However, there are a number of other oil techniques where you will need to allow the first layer of paint to dry before you start. Take care to ensure that this first layer has dried fully, which may take several days. If it is not completely dry any subsequent layers may crack as the underlying paint sucks the oil from the top surface.

Glazing

Essentially a glaze is a thin layer of colour that allows the underlying colours to show through somewhat. You can create a glaze by adding a little colour to some alkyd gel. Allow time to experiment with applying glazes as sometimes several thin glazes (even of different colours) can be more effective than one heavy layer. You will find that a glaze tends to make any underlying colours appear slightly darker. A dark blue glaze is particularly effective to increase the depth and luminosity of shadows.

Scumbling

Scumbling is another way to apply thin layers of translucent colour. To mix a scumble add a little white paint to a coloured glaze. This makes it semi-opaque, so the effect is rather like a coloured mist. Scumbles tend to lighten any areas to which they are applied, so are useful for toning down.

▼ The background hills in this study were a little too strong. See what a difference adding a pale blue scumble over the left-hand side makes to the mood of the picture.

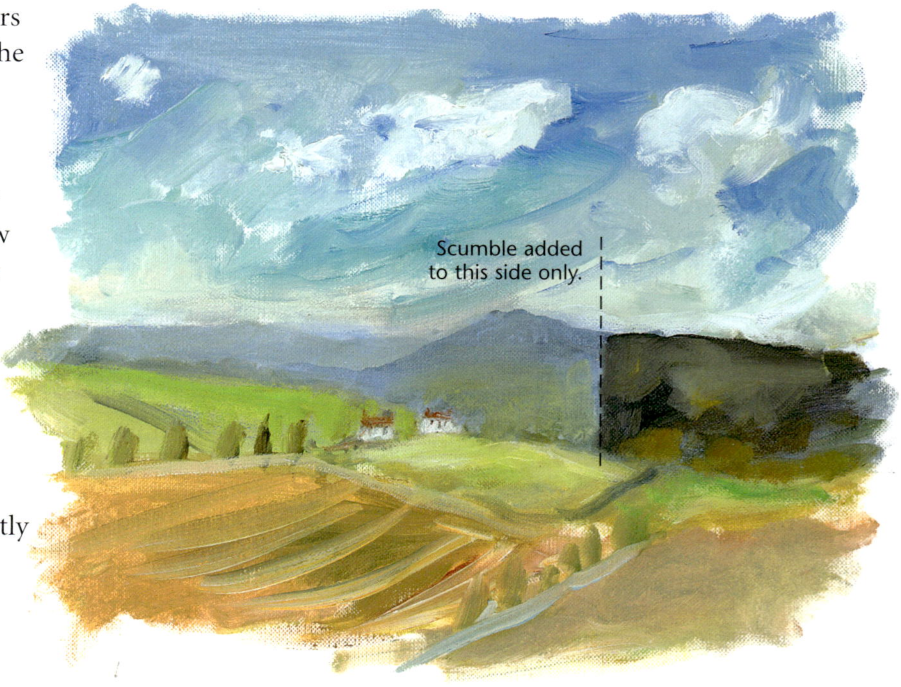

Stippling

Stippling involves painting a broken layer of colour on top of a dry underlayer. This can be either as patches of colour, or as a fairly solid layer brushed over most of the canvas, yet still allowing a little of the underlying colour to show through. You may find stippling useful for painting water ripples.

Dry brush

The technique of dragging a brush loaded with dryish colour across the painting surface is familiar to watercolourists. In oils this can be an equally effective way to paint shimmering water or add interest to a grassy meadow. Practise by using the 12 mm (½ in) brush loaded with plenty of paint but little or no medium. Gently drag the brush across the canvas with fairly light pressure so that a broken strip of colour is left behind.

◀ Top: Cobalt Violet and white were stippled over a dry layer of Yellow Ochre. Bottom: Venetian Red was gently dragged with a dry brush over already dry Yellow Ochre.

▼ **Towards Evening, Chelsea Reach**
25 x 30 cm (10 x 12 in)
To paint the shimmering water I gently stippled Naples Yellow and white over an underpainting of pale pink. Highlights near the bridge are pure white.

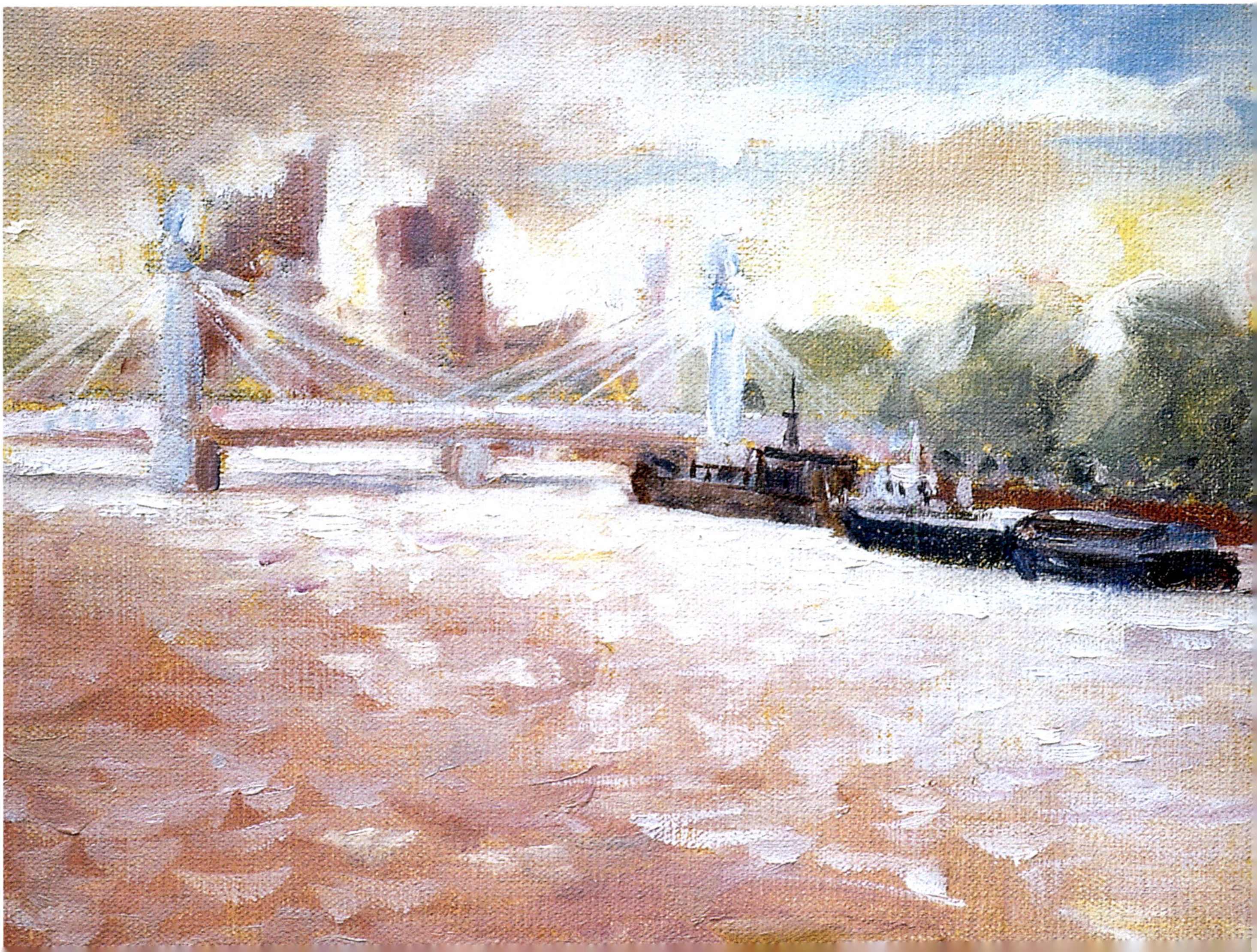

Shape and Form

Being able to imitate a three-dimensional shape on a flat sheet of paper is perhaps the most important lesson to learn when starting to paint. The key point to remember is that it is the contrast of light against dark, and dark against light that enables you, as an artist, to show the shape and form of any object.

Direction of light

In landscape painting there is usually only one light source – the sun. Where light catches one side of an object, it will appear lighter, with the unlit side falling into shadow. The three tree studies painted here each show the source of light coming from a different angle. You can see how this affects the shadows and highlights, and helps to give each tree shape and form.

I often place an arrow on my sketches to indicate the direction of light. It is also helpful to produce a tonal study before starting the actual painting. This acts as a 'plan', showing the main areas of light and shade. By establishing the pattern of lights and darks at the beginning you will avoid problems later on.

To create effective shadows, apply a thin glaze of French Ultramarine.

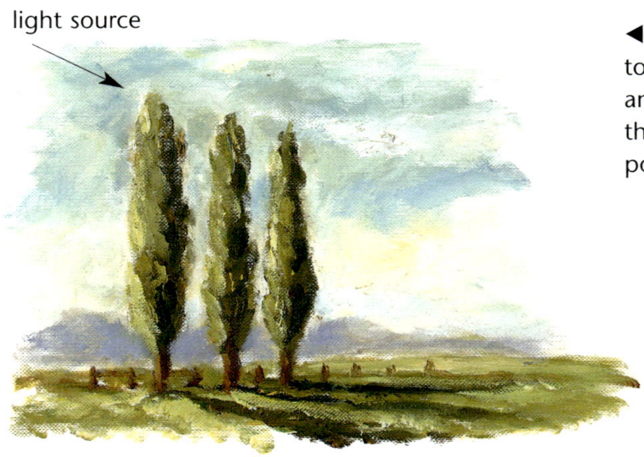

◀ Light from the top left casts long, angled shadows to the right of the poplar trees.

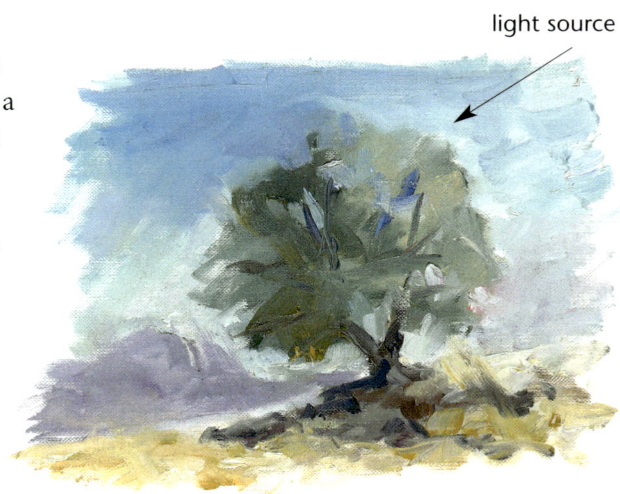

◀ Note how dark the unlit foliage is on this olive tree when the light is from the top right of the picture.

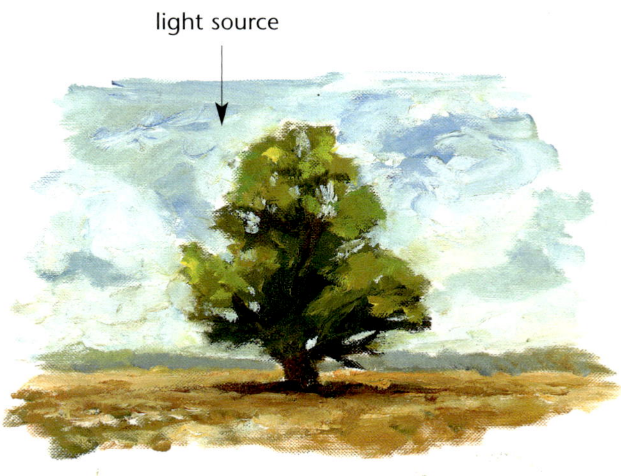

◀ Where the light is overhead only a very small area of shadow appears directly beneath this oak tree. Light also catches the foliage on the upper leaves.

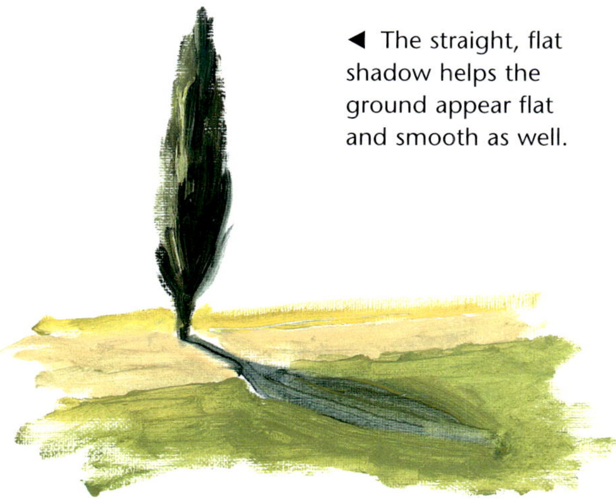

◀ The straight, flat shadow helps the ground appear flat and smooth as well.

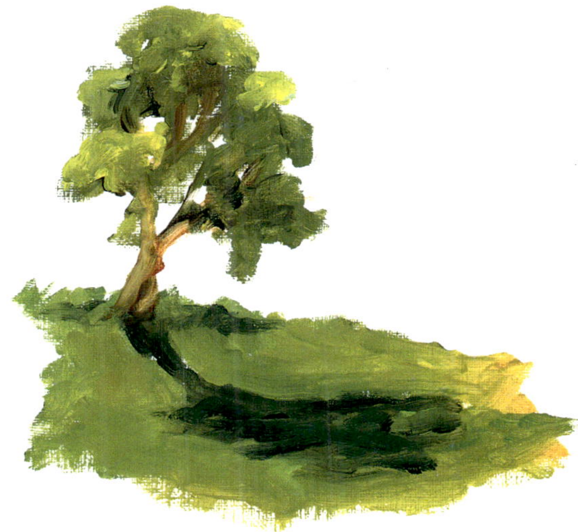

◀ The changing angle of the shadow follows the rounded contours of the bank, making it appear as a steep slope.

Effective use of shadows

Shadows are an important tool for the landscape painter. They can add interest and texture to the foreground, perhaps where a large tree casts its shadow over a footpath or field. They add shape and form to buildings and hedgerows. Even clouds sometimes cast soft shadows onto the open landscape, making interesting patterns of light and dark over fields and hills. An awareness of shadows and how they can enhance the composition of your paintings is another useful point for the landscape painter.

▼ **Late Summer Shadows**
20 x 25 cm (8 x 10 in)
Shadows falling on the stubble make a pattern of light and dark, and describe the field's rough surface.

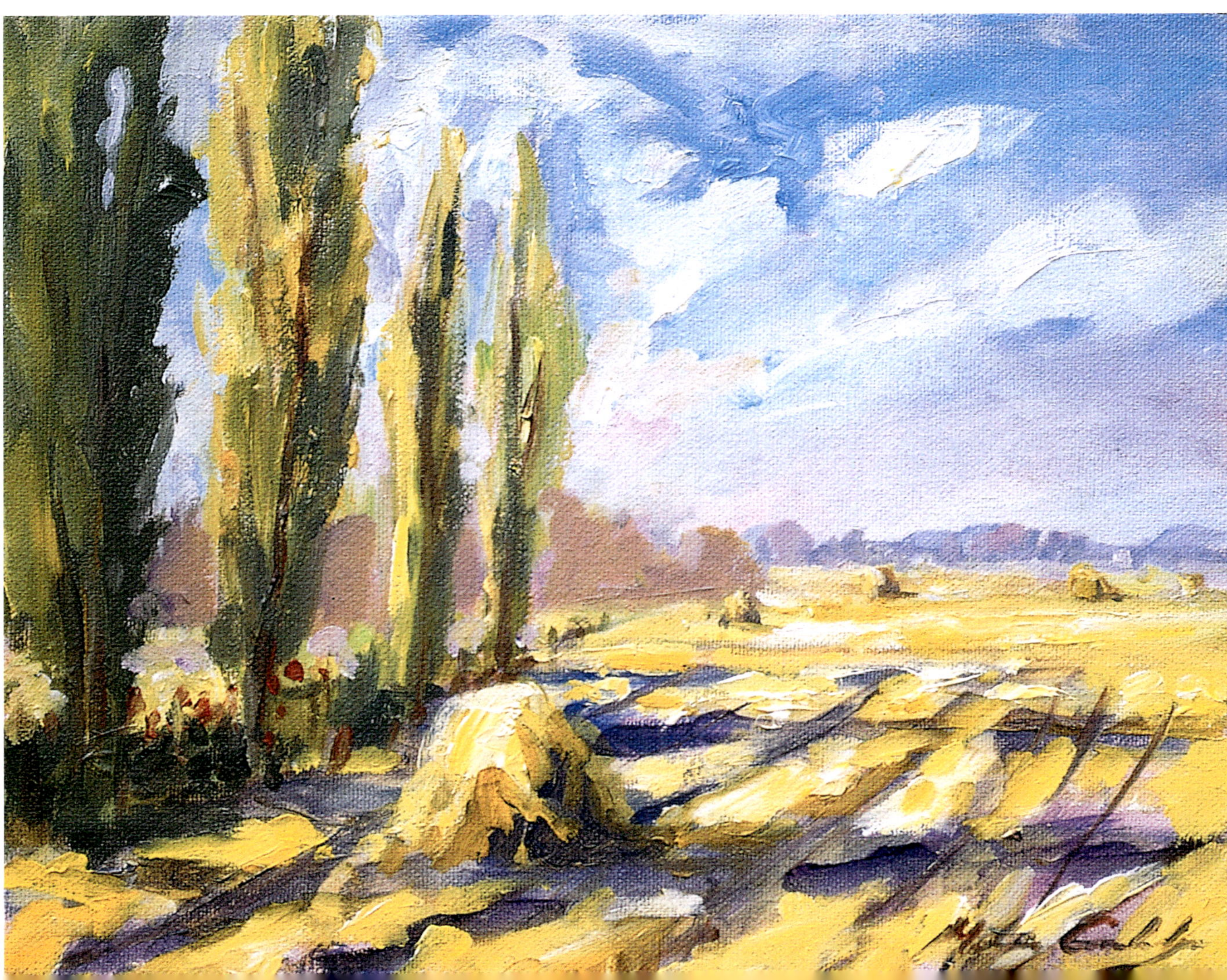

Tonal Values

Artists often speak of 'tone' or 'tonal values'. But what do these terms really mean? Tone or the tonal value of a colour is simply how light or dark the shade of colour is. Every colour has its own tonal range, from full strength to its palest tint. Darker colours tend to break down into more different tones than lighter ones.

A tonal scale

However, another meaning of tonal value for the artist is how relatively light or dark a colour is within a painting. To help you judge tonal values, make a simple tonal scale. Start with pure black and gradually make each step paler by adding white until you reach pure white. Try to have at least five stages. You may find it useful to number each value as an extra guide. Use your tonal scale to look at colours and grade them according to how closely they match the tones on your basic scale.

A tonal scale is also helpful when comparing different colours within a painting. I have painted two studies as an example, the first in colour and the second as a monochrome. Look at each colour alongside your tonal scale to judge the relative light or darkness of each. You may find some surprises. Not all reds and yellows are light in tone.

In the Sepia monochrome study only the difference in tonal values creates the finished painting. Notice how the tree on the far left, which is orange in the colour study, appears as the same dark tone as the green tree alongside it.

▲ A simple tonal scale from black to white.

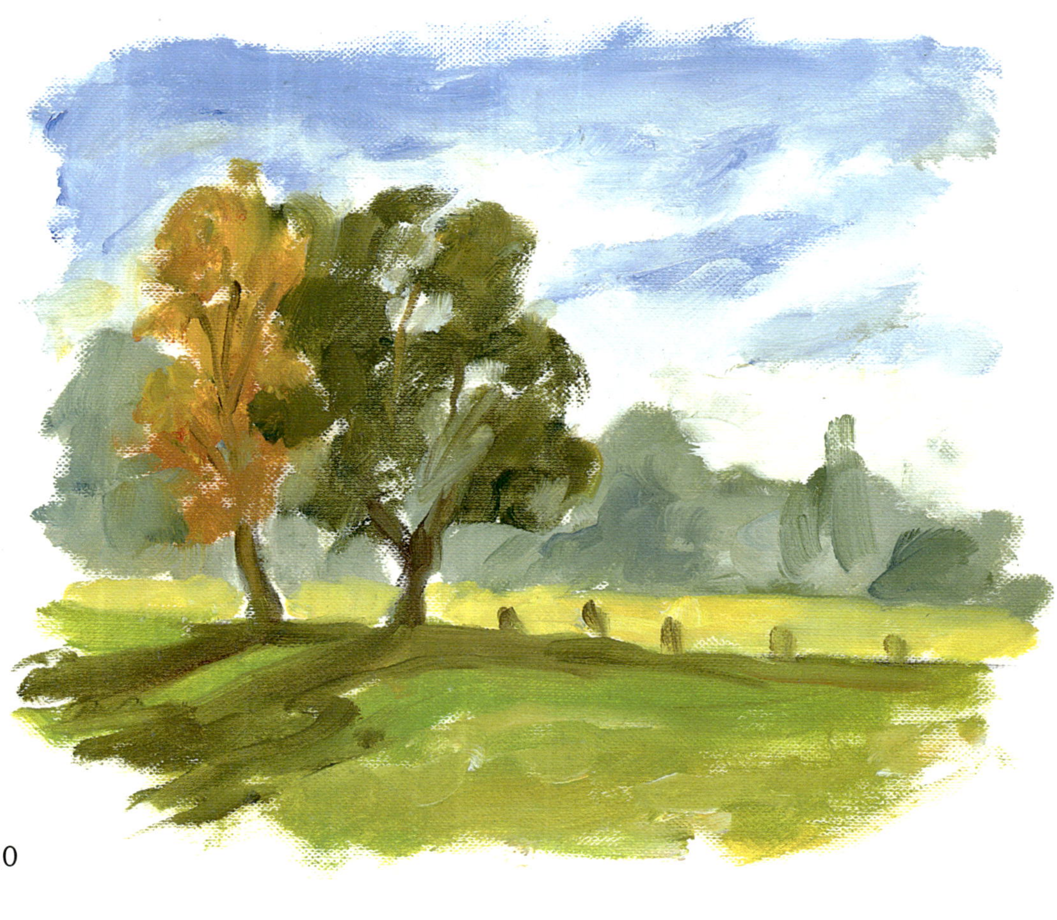

◀ My initial colour study showing the green and orange foliage of the two foreground trees.

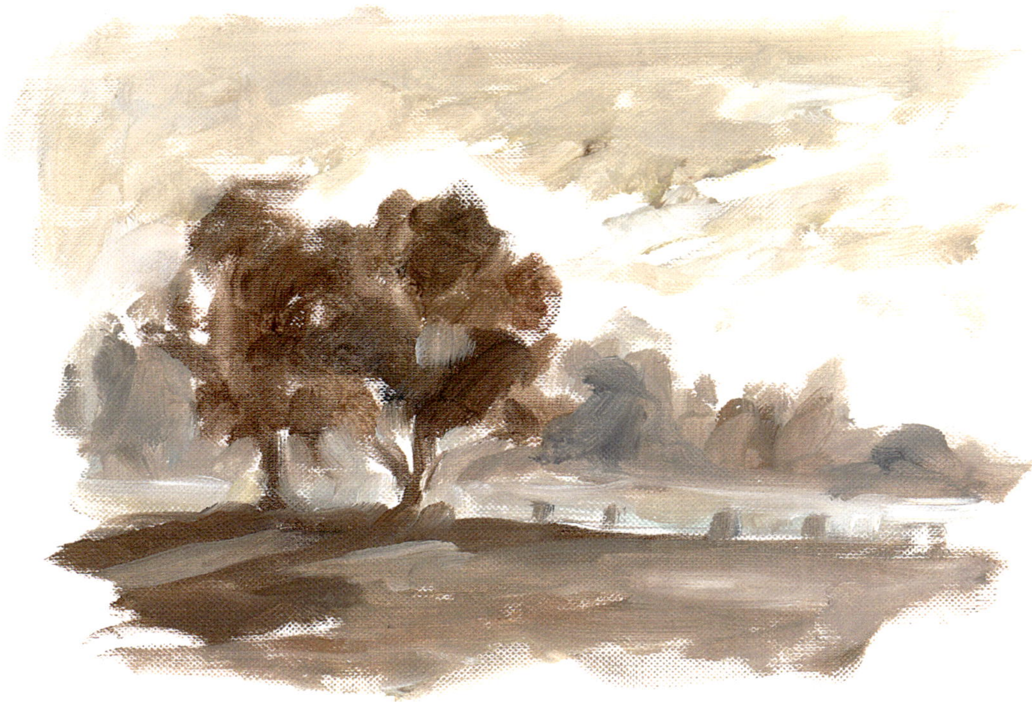

◀ In this monochrome study both foreground trees now appear as the same tone.

Local tone

As well as looking at the relative tone of individual colours, it is important to consider the effect of light on the colour of an object. This gives the local tone, which can be somewhat darker or lighter than the colour of the object. If this sounds complicated, look at my two studies of dogs. One dog is white, the other black. In each case the colour I have painted the dog is not simply pure white or black, but adjusted to what I could actually see. The white dog is mainly darker grey, while the black dog appears relatively pale where the light catches him on his back and tail.

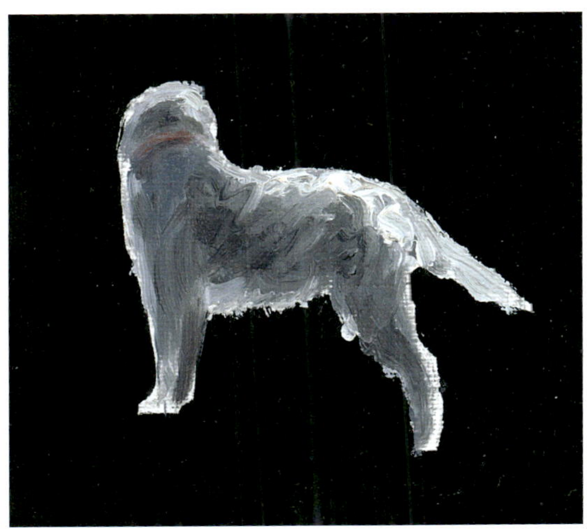

◀ See how the shadows on the white dog appear quite dark. I have painted a black background to help you judge the relative tones of this dog against those of the black one below.

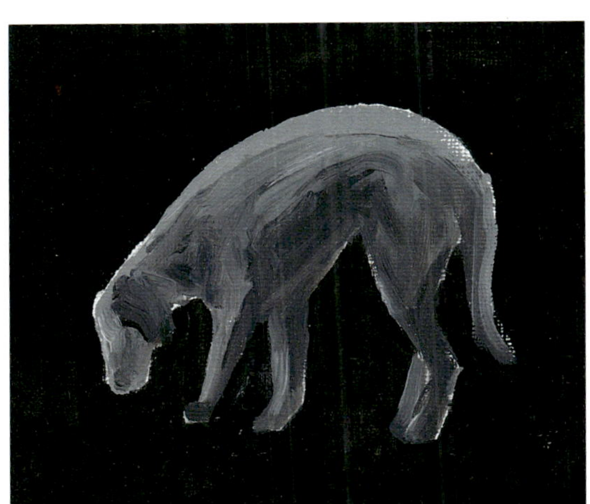

◀ The black dog actually looks very pale where the light catches it. I have added a black background so you can see how light the black dog appears against it.

Paint the colour you actually see rather than the colour you know the object to be.

Creating Depth and Distance

As a landscape painter it is important to be able to create a feeling of depth and distance. There are a number of ways to achieve this. Perhaps the most obvious way to do so is to use compositional elements, such as having a long road leading into the distance, or placing figures or buildings to give a sense of scale. These all rely on an understanding of linear perspective.

Linear perspective

When you are outdoors the horizon line will always fall at your eye level. Horizontal lines above this eyeline appear to bend downwards towards the horizon, whereas those below it will appear to angle upwards. All such lines eventually converge at some far distant point known as the 'vanishing point'. This is most obvious if you look at a railway track. The rails appear to converge at the point where they meet the horizon.

You will notice that not all angles converge at a vanishing point within the frame of your painting. Some angles are so slight as to carry on for a considerable distance beyond the canvas or paper, but all will eventually meet the horizon.

▼ Breezy Morning, Brightlingsea
20 x 30 cm (8 x 12 in)
This view has several aspects that help create a sense of distance. The yacht on the left leads you into the painting, while the clouds in the sky recede towards the horizon. The distant shoreline was painted in a soft grey tone to help push it into the far distance.

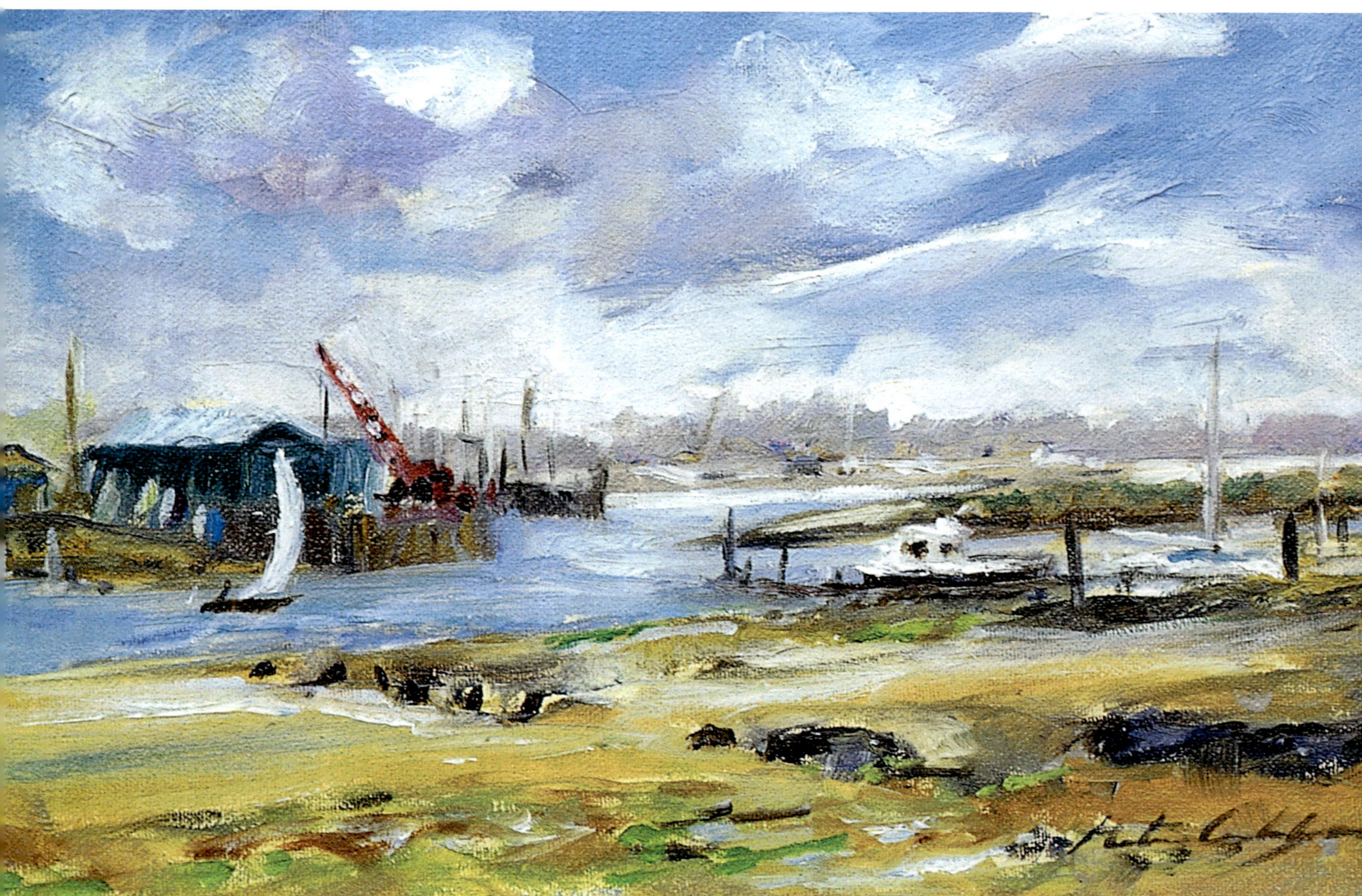

When you place the horizon line in your painting it is important to apply the basic rule of linear perspective. If you are having problems making a row of trees or a bridge look 'right', first check whether or not the object is above or below your horizon line. Then ask yourself if you have correctly angled the edges of the bridge, building or row of trees upwards or downwards as appropriate for the viewpoint.

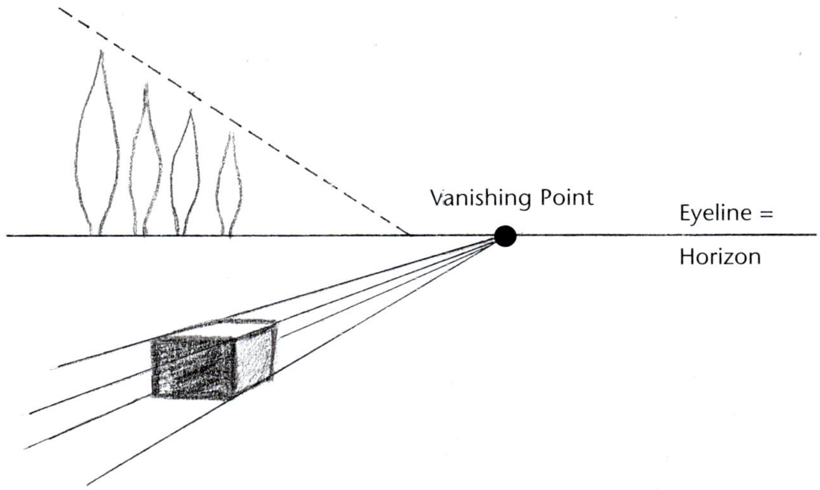

▲ Use this diagram to remind you of the basic rule – lines above the horizon angle downwards towards it, while lines below the horizon angle upwards towards it.

Creating scale

Apart from understanding the principles of linear perspective, there are a number of other points to bear in mind when working out the correct scale for different features in your paintings. If you decide to include buildings in your composition, take care to ensure that any figures in the same plane can fit through the doorways. If you wish to portray figures walking along a road and into the distance, make sure the heads all relate to the same horizontal line – unless you have a very low or very high viewpoint.

Paths should gradually become narrower as they go towards the horizon to give a sense of scale and any buildings alongside them should be in scale. This is easy to achieve by using the road width as your basic measure. If the height of a building in the foreground is twice the width of the road alongside it, then this same measure can be used to work out the correct scale for buildings in the background of your painting.

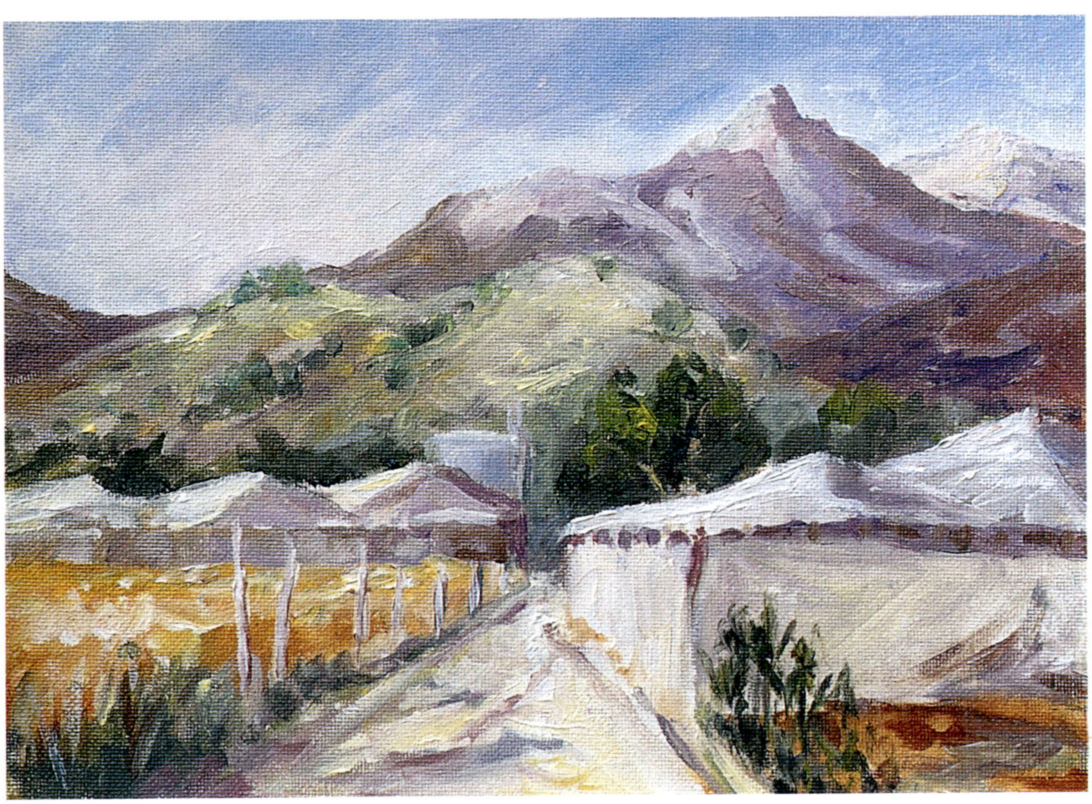

◀ **Farm Track, Sierra Nevada**
23 x 30 cm (9 x 12 in)
Painted on location, the mountains appeared pink and pale mauve in the early evening light. The farm track leads the eye into the painting, while the receding building also helps create a sense of depth.

Aerial perspective

Exaggerating the effects of atmosphere can also create an impression of distance in a painting. A knowledge of aerial perspective, where distant features look paler and bluer, is a useful means of creating both mood and recession in a composition. Balancing colour overall or setting a 'colour key' can also enhance the feeling you want to convey.

A misty morning is an excellent time to learn about aerial perspective. The effect of the intervening atmosphere is at its most obvious. Distant hills appear very pale indeed, and even trees in the middle distance can look much bluer and with less detail than on a clear day. This awareness of atmosphere and its effect on distant views is particularly important on a sunny day when the visible effect is much less. However, in order for your painting to look right you will still need to use artistic licence and remember to soften distant objects and also paint them a little bluer and paler than they actually appear.

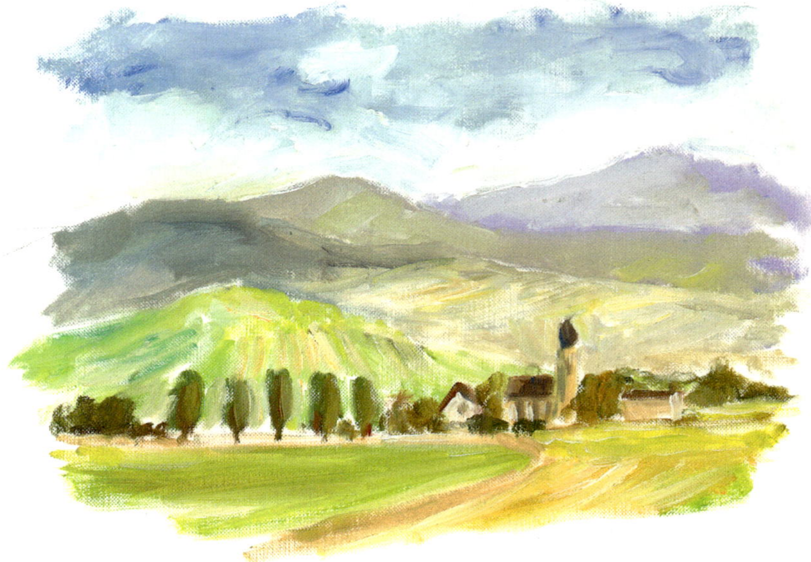

▲ Even though this study was made on a sunny day the background hills were painted much softer to help them recede into the distance.

Colour key

It is important to set the overall colour key for the mood and atmosphere for a painting from the outset. A high-key painting is one where the colours and tones give a general feeling of warmth. A sunny beach scene or a field of golden corn in the sunshine would be ideal subjects for a high-key painting.

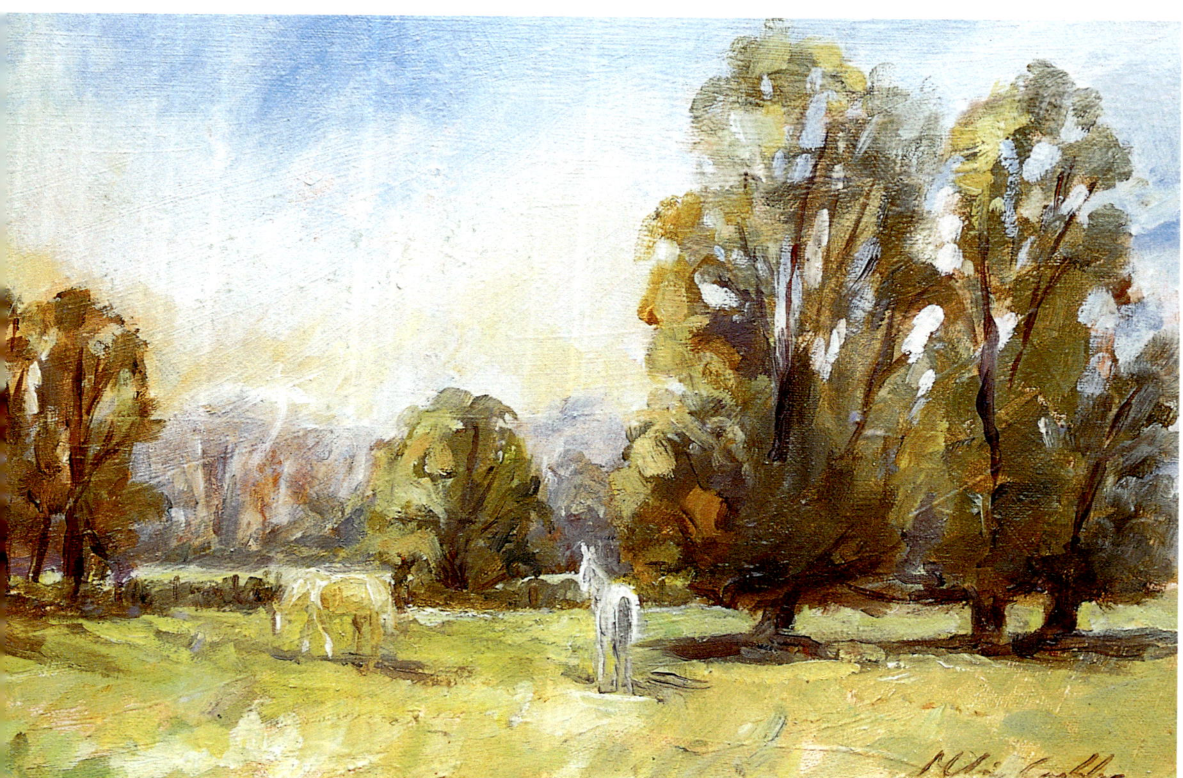

◀ **Early Morning Grazers**
28 x 36 cm (11 x 14 in)
In the soft light of early morning the horses appeared almost ghostlike in the pale landscape.

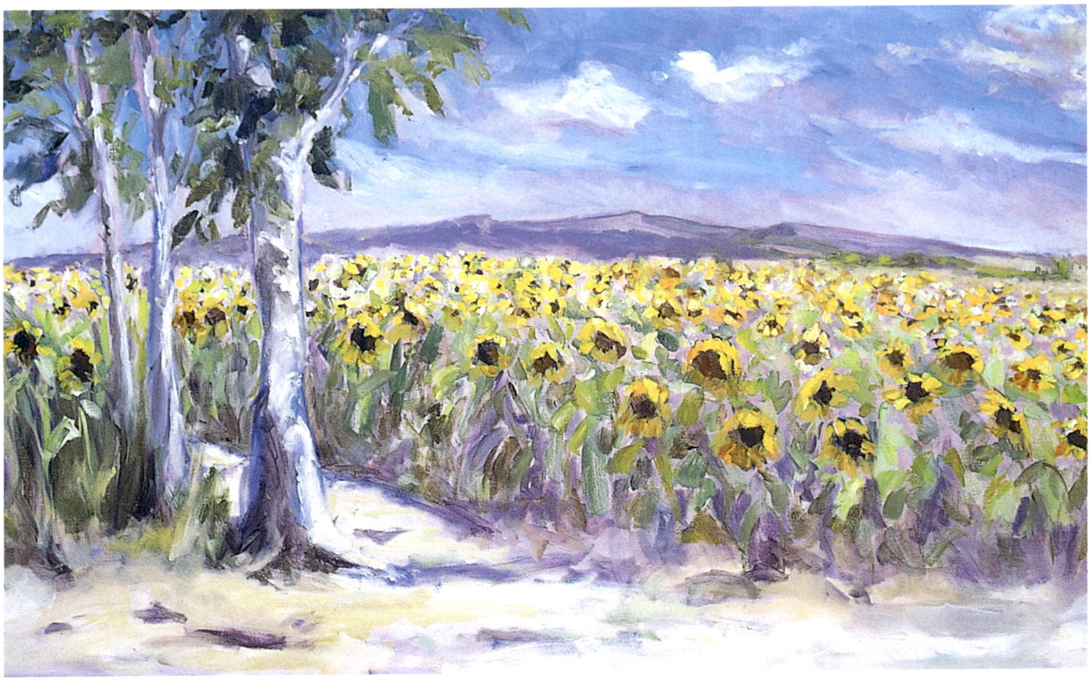

◀ **Sunflowers near Benon**
30 x 41 cm (12 x 16 in)
In this high-key painting most of the colours are at the brighter end of the scale. Even the shadows are light and airy.

The colours and tones that make up a low-key painting are at the lower end of the tonal scale. Such paintings can be dark and mysterious, but it is important not to paint them too dark. Dusky landscapes or interiors can make excellent subjects for low-key paintings.

High-key colour

To capture a high-key mood in your landscape, choose mainly lighter tones and brighter colours. Take care not to paint any shadows too dark as this can upset the overall balance of the painting. Keep strong contrasts to a minimum. Working with paler colours in oils generally means adding white paint to each mix, but again do not overdo this as your painting can appear chalky rather than bright and light. Use pure colours when possible, such as Naples Yellow, adding white only when you really need to use it.

Low-key colour

A low-key painting contains many darker tones and only a few patches of brighter colour. Work with soft, darker greys, purples and blues, blending them together to create the atmosphere you require. However, try to keep some of the darkest tones fairly thin. Reserve thicker paint for lighter areas, otherwise the general effect can be dark and deadened with too much heavy paint. Do not be afraid to add just a couple of touches of bright colour to stand out against all the greys. These touches of colour can lead the eye through the painting – as, for example, patches of light on a sunlit path through a dark woodland. Or highlight the main focal point such as a figure or an animal.

▼ **Evening Stables**
28 x 36 cm (11 x 14 in)
Most tones are at the lower end of the scale in this quiet rural scene. As a result the few highlights are very effective.

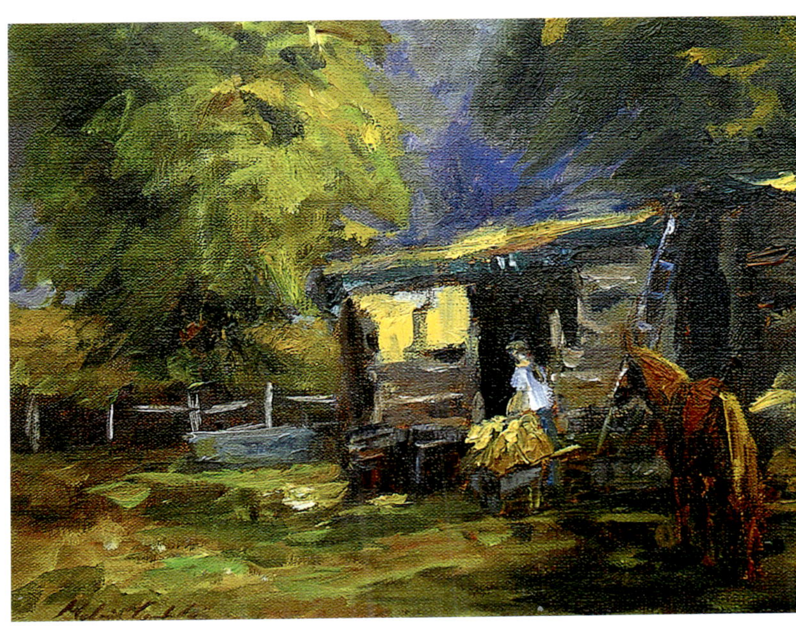

Planning your Paintings

What makes a good painting? Many elements are obviously involved, and these can be different for different artists. However, here are some key points.

As well as an interesting range of tones try to have a good overall composition and to keep objects in proportion to each other. Composition simply describes the arrangement of objects within a painting. Before starting the main painting make a quick sketch or tonal study to help you understand how the overall composition will look. Do the lights and darks balance each other? Is the centre or focus of interest obvious and does any path or river lead the viewer's eye towards it? These are basic considerations, but they should help you plan an interesting and successful painting and they are worth thinking about and planning carefully in advance.

Composition

The first, and most important, point to decide is where to place the main focus of interest for your landscape. This might be a building, boat, figure or tree. One rule that may help you is the 'rule of thirds'. Start by dividing your canvas into three equal horizontal and vertical sections, resulting in four points at which these lines intersect.

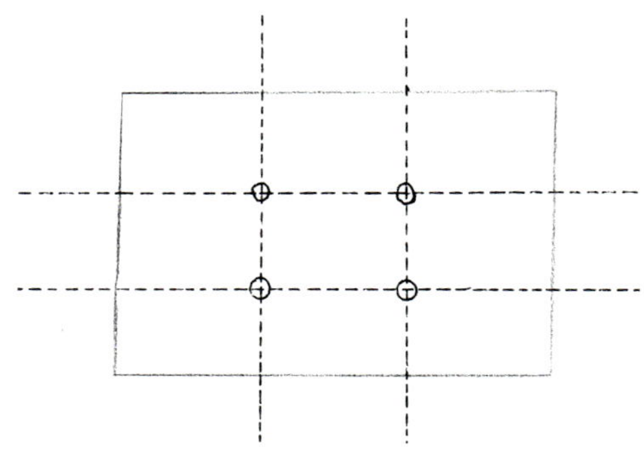

◀ The 'rule of thirds', showing the four intersecting points. Place the focus of interest in your painting at one of these points.

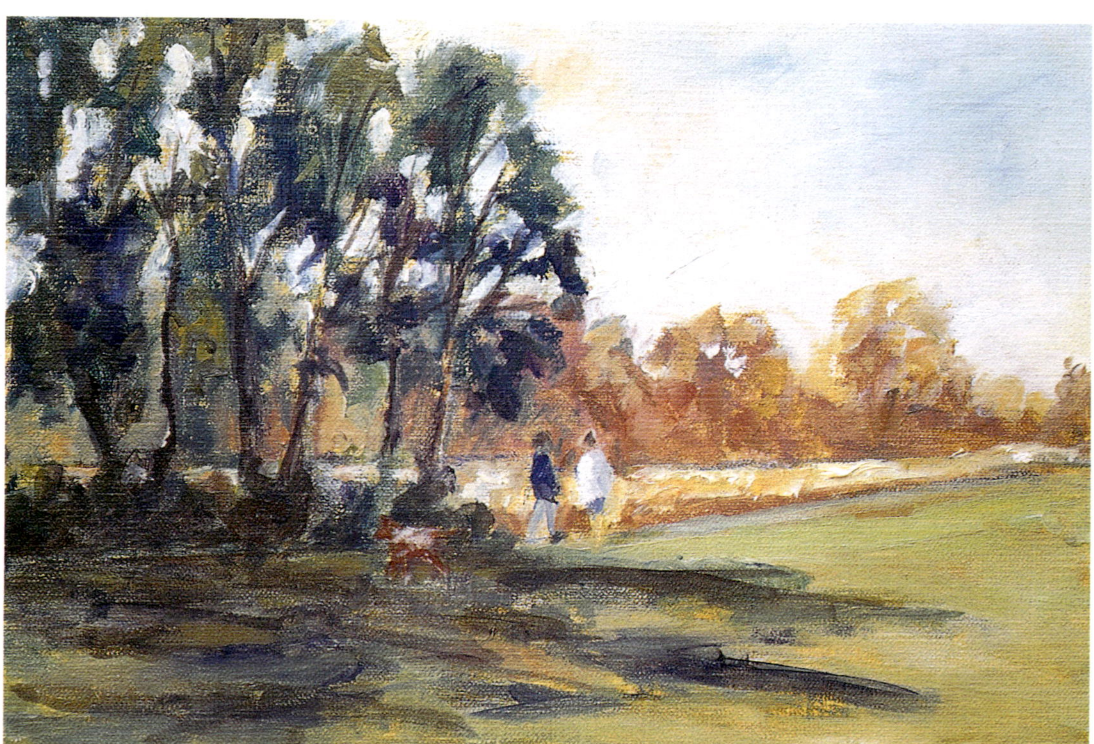

◀ **Walking the Dogs, North Downs**
28 x 36 cm (11 x 14 in)
I have used a simple 'L' shape composition to lead the eye to the two figures by placing them at the apex of the 'L' where the trees and shadows meet.

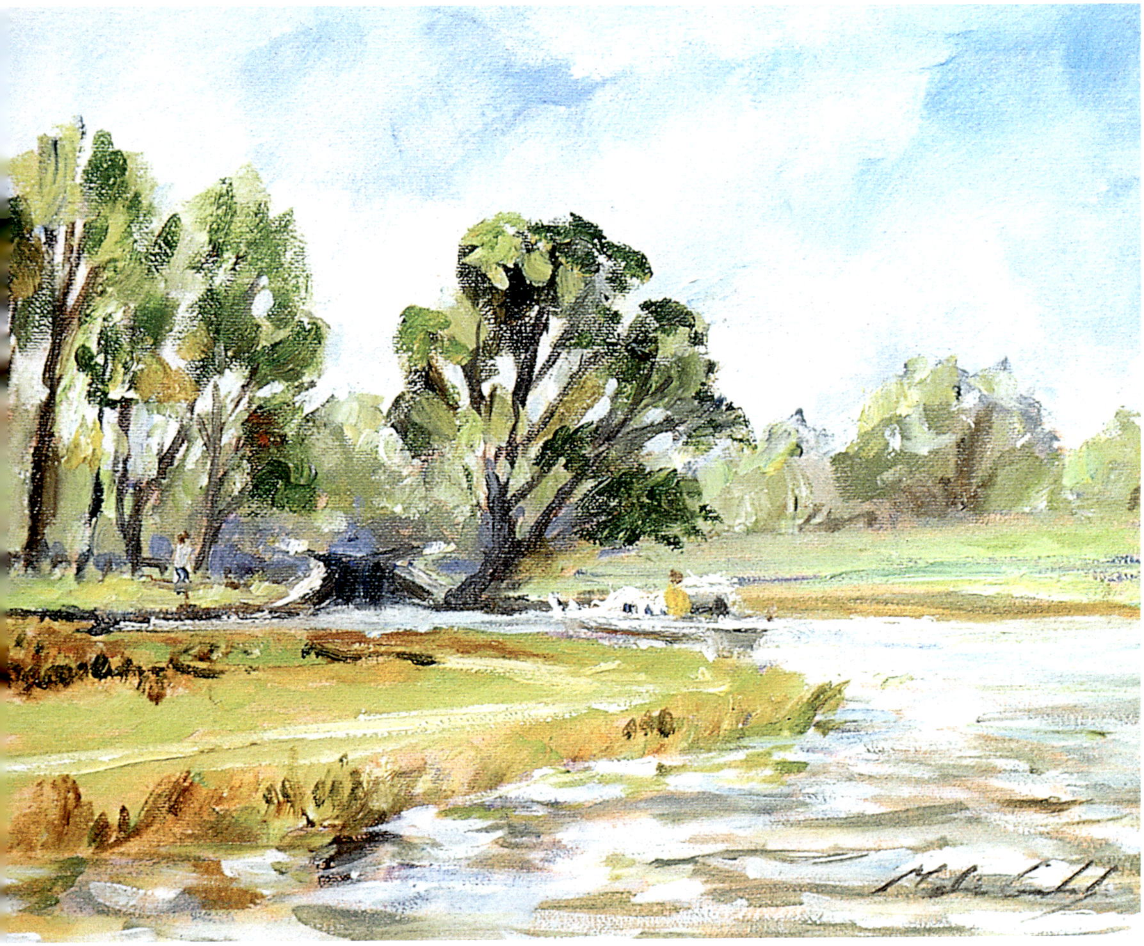

◄ Cruising Along
25 x 30 cm (10 x 12 in)
The bend in the river leads the eye up to the lock gates, which are the principal point of interest.

▼ Through the Olives
20 x 24 cm (8 x 9½ in)
The road leads the eye into this painting and on around the mountain, leaving the viewer to wonder what lies around the corner.

Each of these intersections occurs at a point that gives proportions that are termed the 'golden section'. By placing your point of interest on, or fairly near to, any of these intersections you will be well on your way to creating a good overall composition for your landscape.

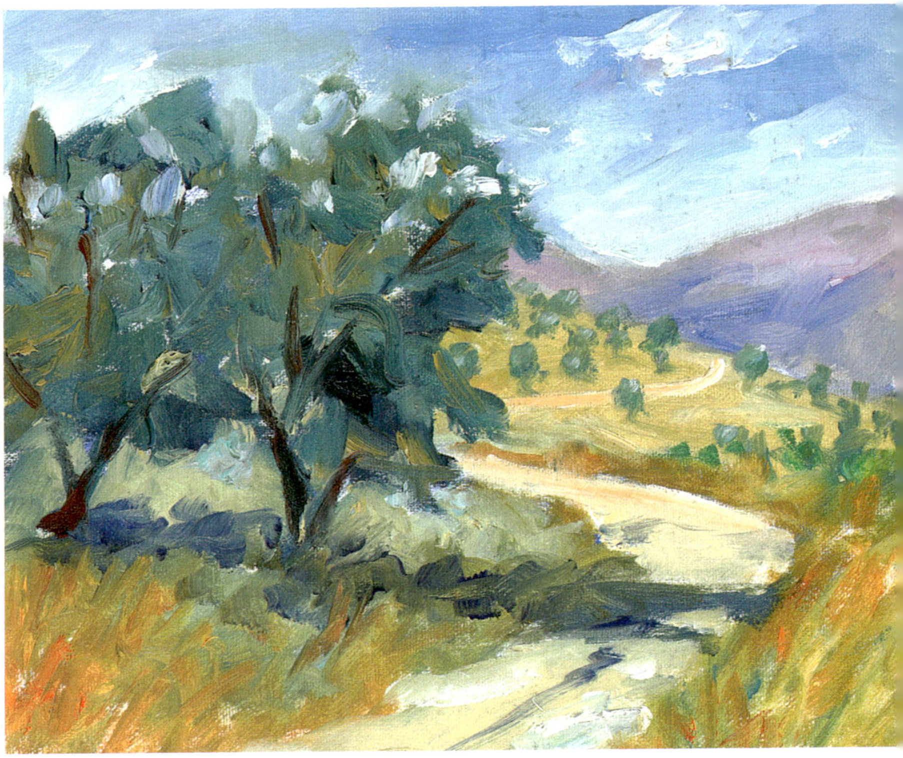

Leading the viewer

Another way to help the structure of a painting is to include a pathway of some sort to guide the viewer's eye to the main point of interest. This could be a simple track or path, or a river, or even plough lines in a field. Whatever you use, take care not to lead the viewer's eye beyond the edge of the painting. For instance, curve a path back or add a strong feature that will act as a 'stopper' to hold the viewer's attention within the confines of the painting.

Common pitfalls

There are several standard compositional shapes, which can be a useful starting point when planning a painting. Here are some of the more common pitfalls, with my suggested standard solutions alongside. In each case a simple alteration, such as moving a path or exaggerating one feature, can considerably improve the composition by creating a successful and pleasing arrangement rather than one that discourages the viewer.

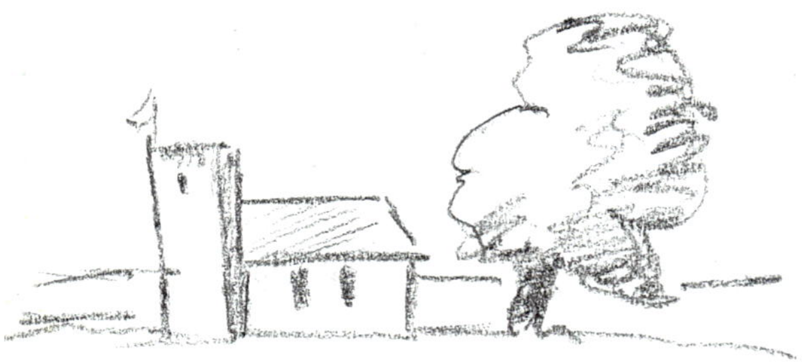

◀ Having two equal points of interest tends to encourage the viewer to flick visually from one to the other.

▶ Here I have emphasized the tree on the right by making it larger and added a shadow underneath to reiterate this area as the point of interest.

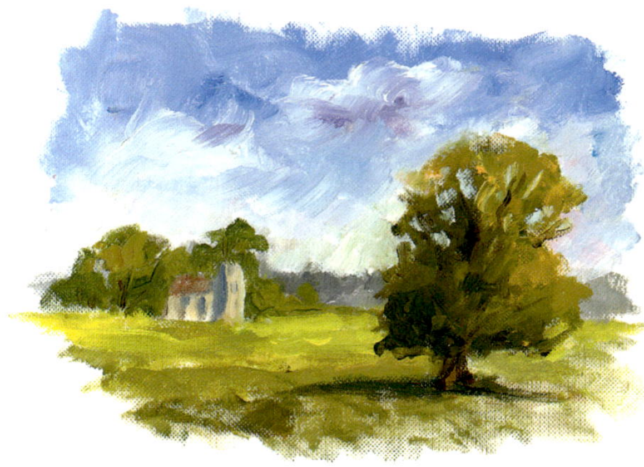

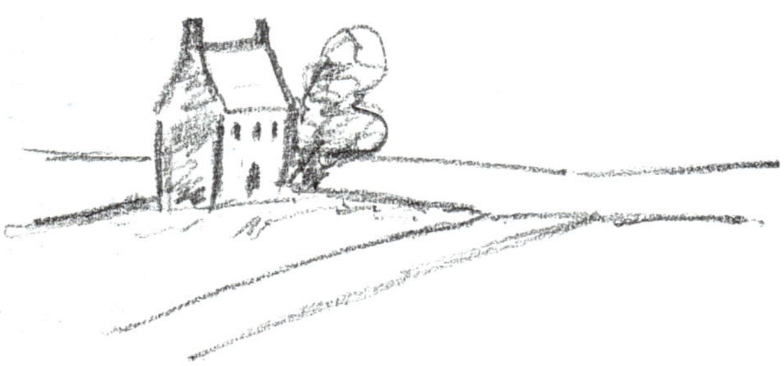

◀ The footpath leads past the cottage and takes the viewer's eye right out of the picture.

▶ Changing the path to a softer 'S' shape that goes to the cottage leads the eye to the main point of focus and keeps the viewer's interest within the picture.

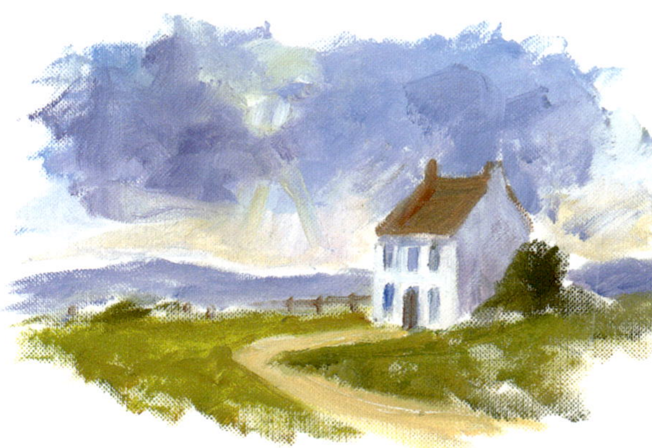

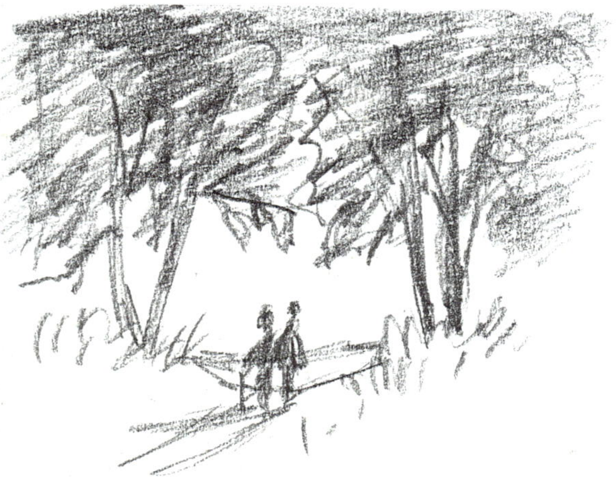

◀ While a circular composition can be exciting, placing the main interest in the absolute centre is somewhat predictable.

▶ Moving the figures to the right and making the circular space of the overhanging trees more oval has considerably improved movement within the composition.

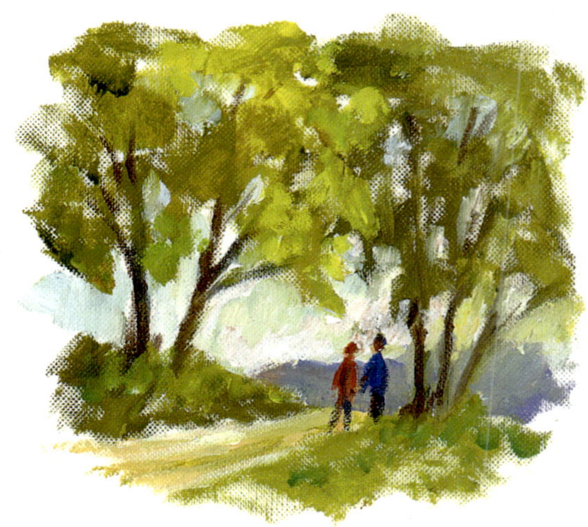

Alternative compositions

Looking beyond standard compositional shapes, as you become more confident in planning your paintings you will probably wish to experiment. Perhaps you may choose an unusual viewpoint to try to make your paintings more exciting and interesting. While there are a few points to avoid, such as splitting the canvas into two equal halves or placing the point of interest at the absolute centre, all of these 'rules' have been broken to good effect at some stage by most artists. Do not be afraid to experiment with your compositions for pictures – you can always go back to the tried and tested ones later on.

I particularly enjoy varying the horizon line in my compositions. Either placing this at the very top of the canvas or even doing away with it altogether for a cliff-top view can be an exciting challenge.

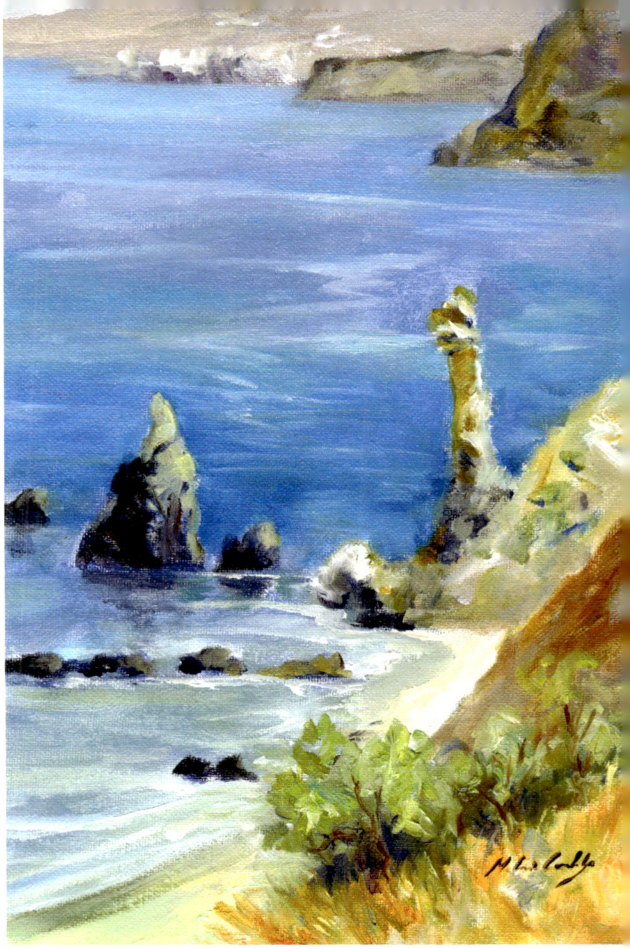

▶ Stone Stacks, Costa Del Sol
36 x 25 cm (14 x 10 in)
This view of the cliffs beyond Nerja in Spain was painted from the car park looking downwards. I placed the horizon at the very top of the canvas to accentuate the feeling of height.

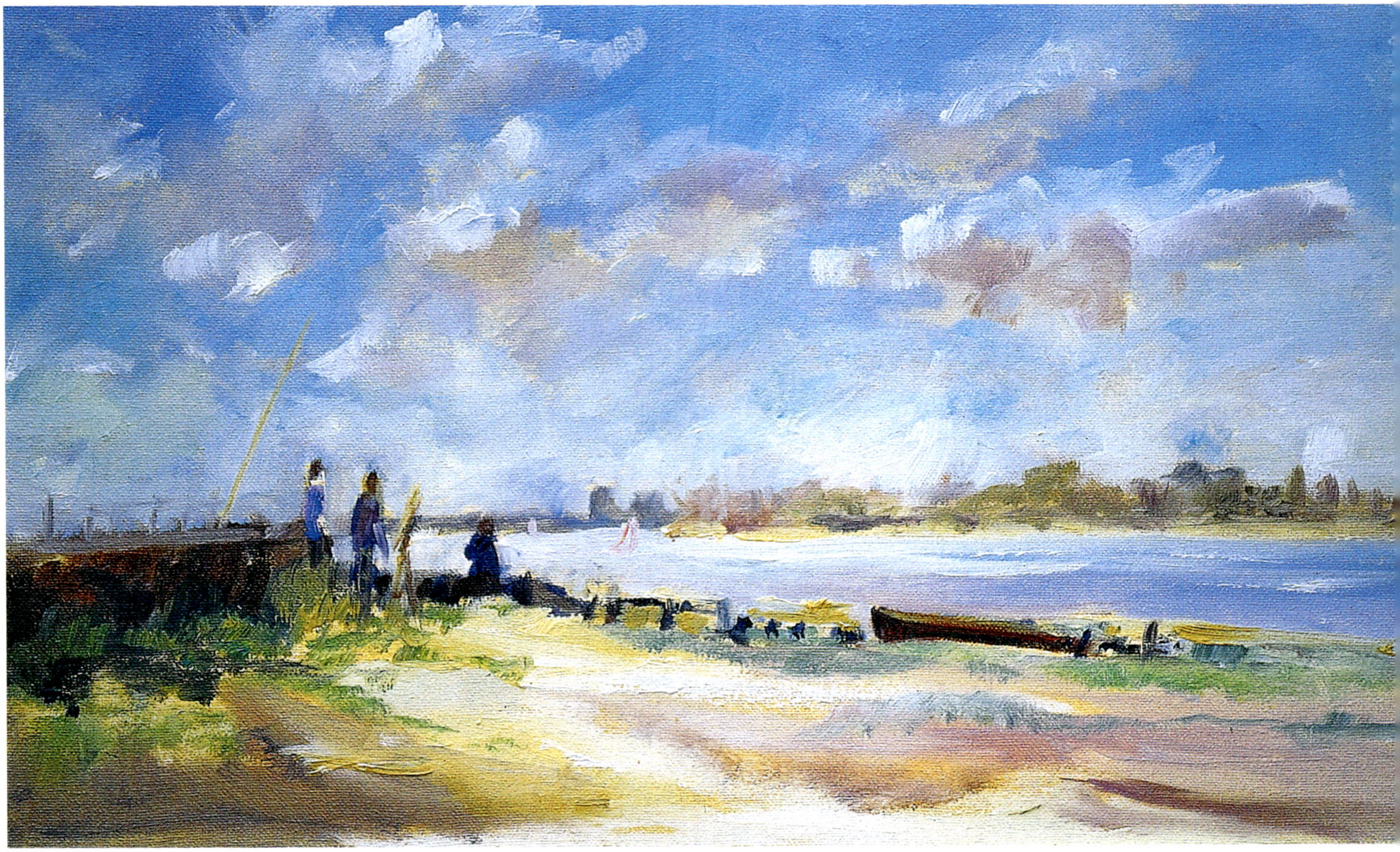

▼ The Plein Air Painters
25 x 36 cm (10 x 14 in)
When painting a mainly horizontal composition, make sure you include at least one vertical element to break through the horizon.

Painting from Photographs

Some artists consider it is out of the question even to think of using a camera as they feel it is cheating. However, I believe that if there is a tool at your disposal, why not use it? The key to working successfully from photographs is to use your camera as an addition to your sketchbook, not a replacement for it. It can be very tempting simply to leave your sketchbook at home and take the camera instead. I know, I did it myself many years ago! It does not take very long to realize just how disappointing photographs can be and how much you wish you had made a quick sketch as well. So please, think of your camera as an extra tool and use it accordingly. This way the sort of photographs you do take should gradually build into a useful library of ideas and detail information, which is a wonderful additional source to have. A camera is especially useful, however, on cold winter days when going out with a sketchbook or paintbox is less appealing.

▼ I used this photograph of a traditional Wey barge as the starting point for the painting below. I particularly liked the effect of the light behind the figures and barge.

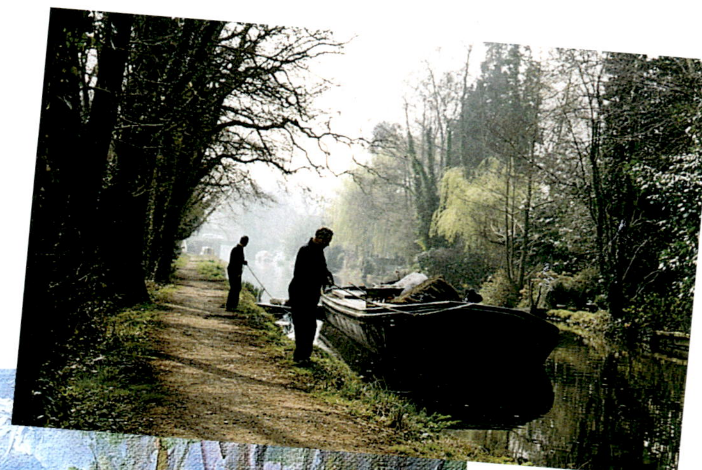

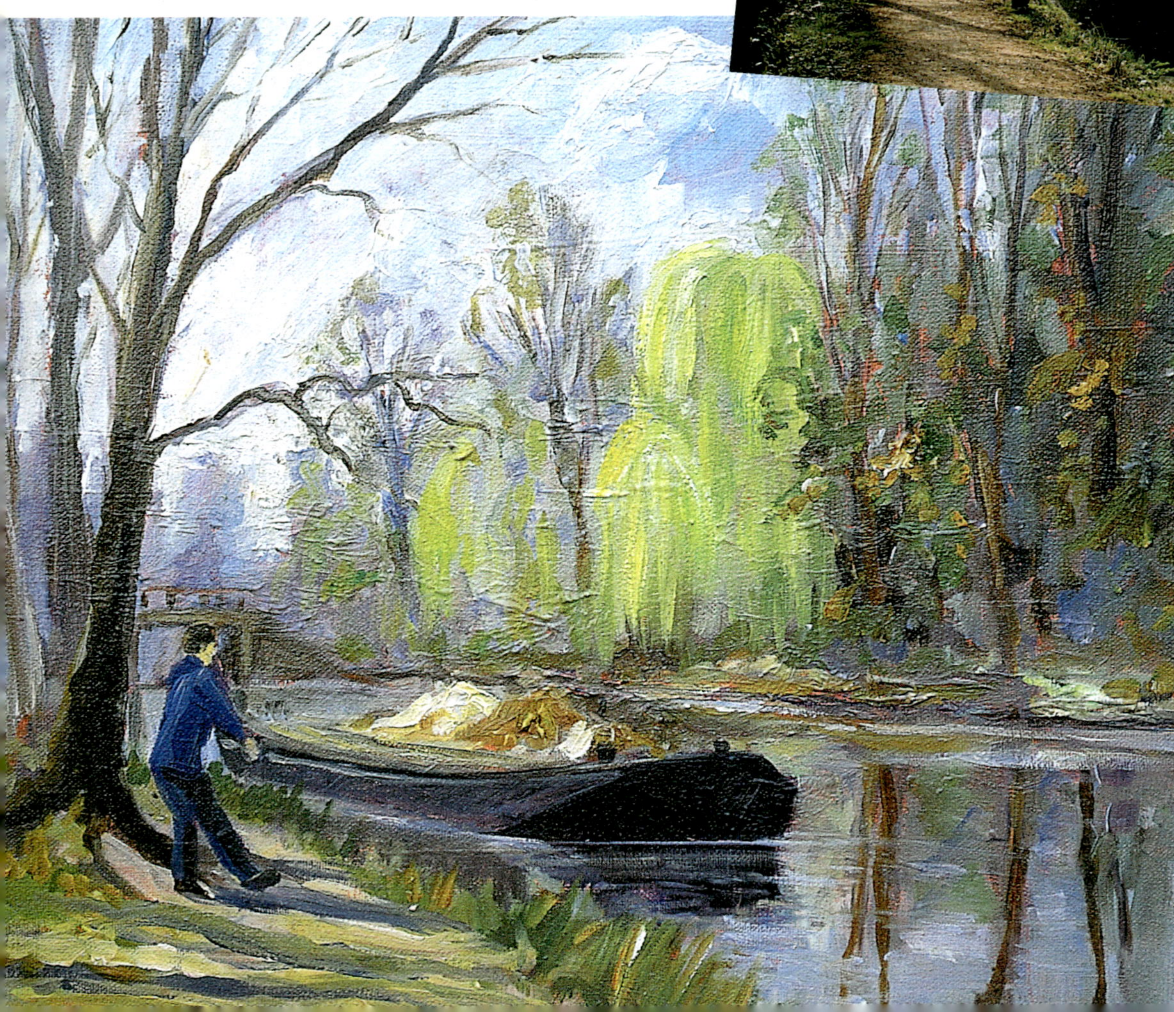

◀ **Wey Barge, Woodham Junction**
30 x 30 cm (12 x 12 in)
In the finished painting I decided to have only one figure since including the second one seemed to crowd the composition. I also changed the position of the figure to give more feeling of movement as he leaned forward on the towpath to pull the barge along.

In order to help you get the most from your camera I have tried to show you how I use mine, usually as a starting point for a painting. Very rarely does the finished painting exactly match the photograph that gave me the idea in the first place! If you can learn to see your photographs in this way, then you should find them useful for ideas and inspiration, rather than simply images to copy slavishly.

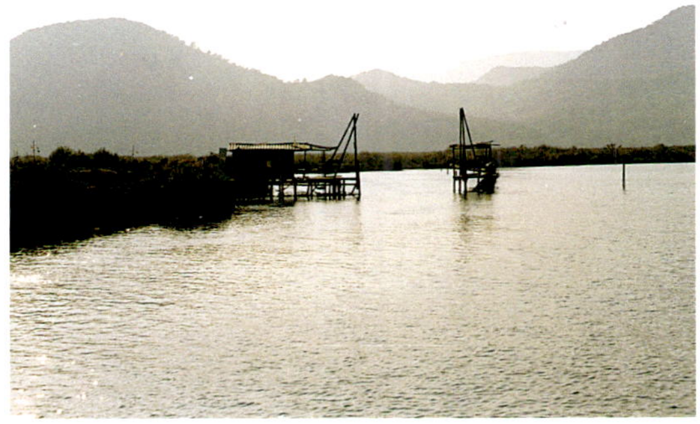

◀ I took this image of fishing huts near Dalyan, Turkey, into the sunlight while enjoying a holiday trip up the Dalyan Estuary. Being on a river cruise with lots of other tourists meant a quick photo was all there was time for!

Using your camera effectively

In order to use a camera effectively it is helpful to be aware of the potential pitfalls of working from photographs as well as the advantages. The camera tends to flatten out the image, bringing colour tones closer together. This point should be borne in mind particularly when photographing open landscapes, since it makes it difficult to discern between different features in the middle and far distance. For this reason I prefer to make a sketch of any open landscape, noting in any details towards the horizon. The camera also tends to blend colours together, which can result in a murky indistinct smudge on the horizon.

However, for making a quick record of details or complicated subjects a camera is ideal. While you may have a moment or two for a quick sketch, if you are with friends or family there is rarely time to sit for half an hour or more to make a detailed drawing. This is where the camera can be most useful. Take several shots of any such subjects from different angles and a few close-up ones of any particular features you might wish to include.

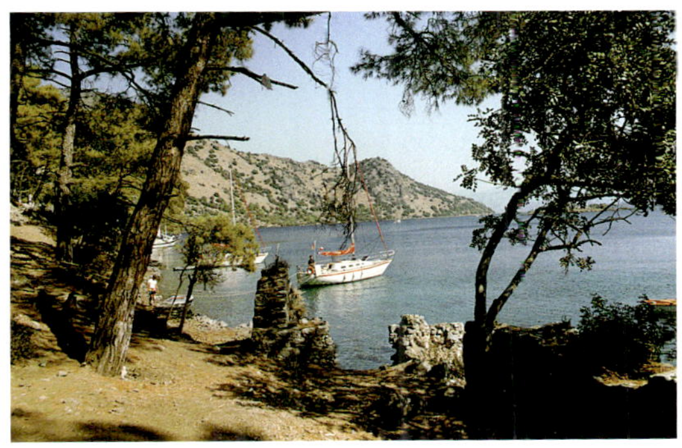

◀ With more time to spare, I was able to walk around to frame the view for this shot of a boat. Provided that the circular composition is offset so that the yacht is not in the dead centre it should make a pleasing painting.

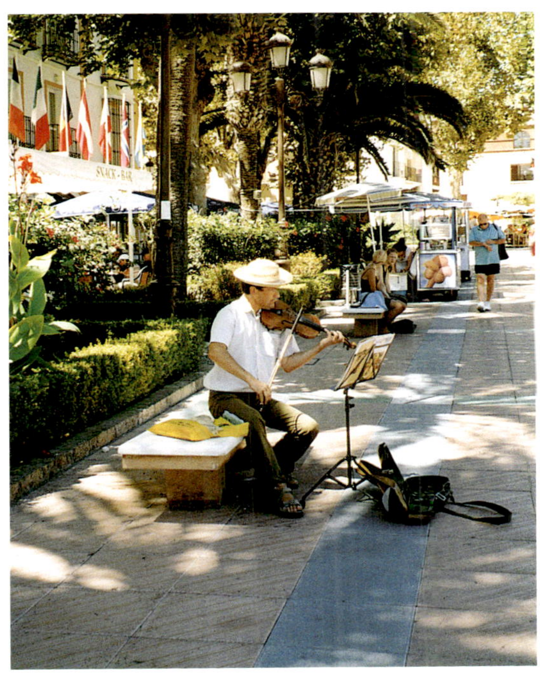

◀ This photograph of a musician on the Balcon de Europa, Nerja, Spain, shows typical use for my camera.

People and animals

For recording figures and animals, however, I suggest you use a camera with caution. It can be a useful aid, but often the results are disappointing. Figures caught on camera are rarely in a natural pose, and I find myself referring back much more to the few quick sketches made on location instead. Try both and see which you prefer, but do not use the camera as an excuse not to sketch at all. After all, sketching is a key way in which we develop as artists.

Using photographs effectively

Having obtained a suitable photograph, let us look at ways of using it effectively as the basis for a successful painting. One point to consider is whether or not to crop the image for a more pleasing composition. To help you decide, cut out two 'L' shapes in white paper and use these to cover over parts of the photograph. It is surprising just how much you can change the composition by using a 'viewfinder' like this.

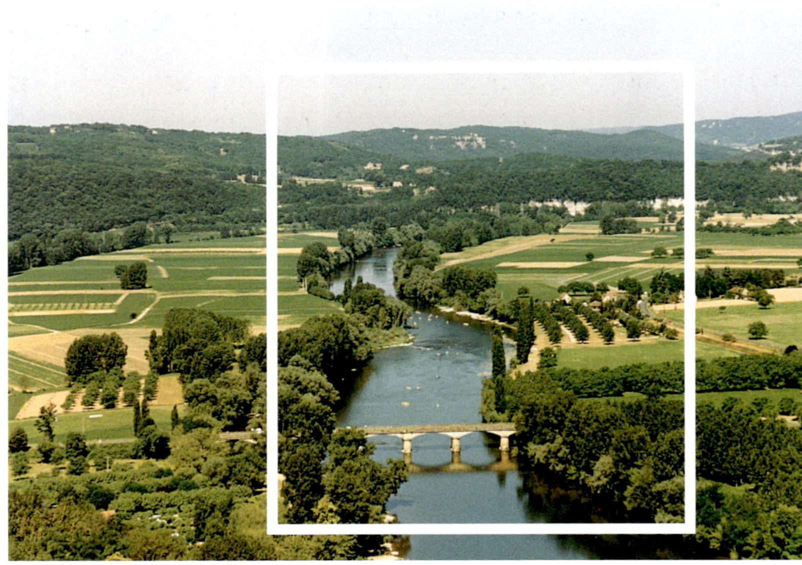

▲ By cropping this view of the Dordogne landscape in France the river becomes the central theme, making an interesting 'S' shape composition.

Initial studies

Having chosen your photograph, make a quick colour study before starting your main painting. This will help you to resolve some of the differences between a photograph and a painting, and to plan how the finished painting will look. Many points may differ between your photograph and the finished painting and I encourage you to do this very useful exercise to decide what should be included. Try a study at least for the first few times you paint directly from photographs.

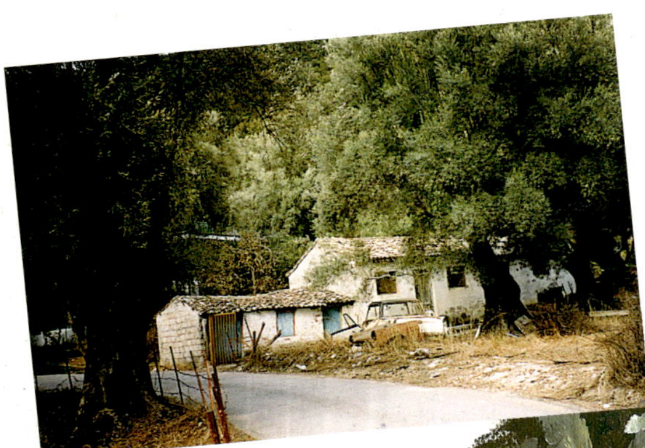

▲ This photograph of a blue-painted hut in Lefkas, Greece, did not fully capture the image as I seemed to remember it.

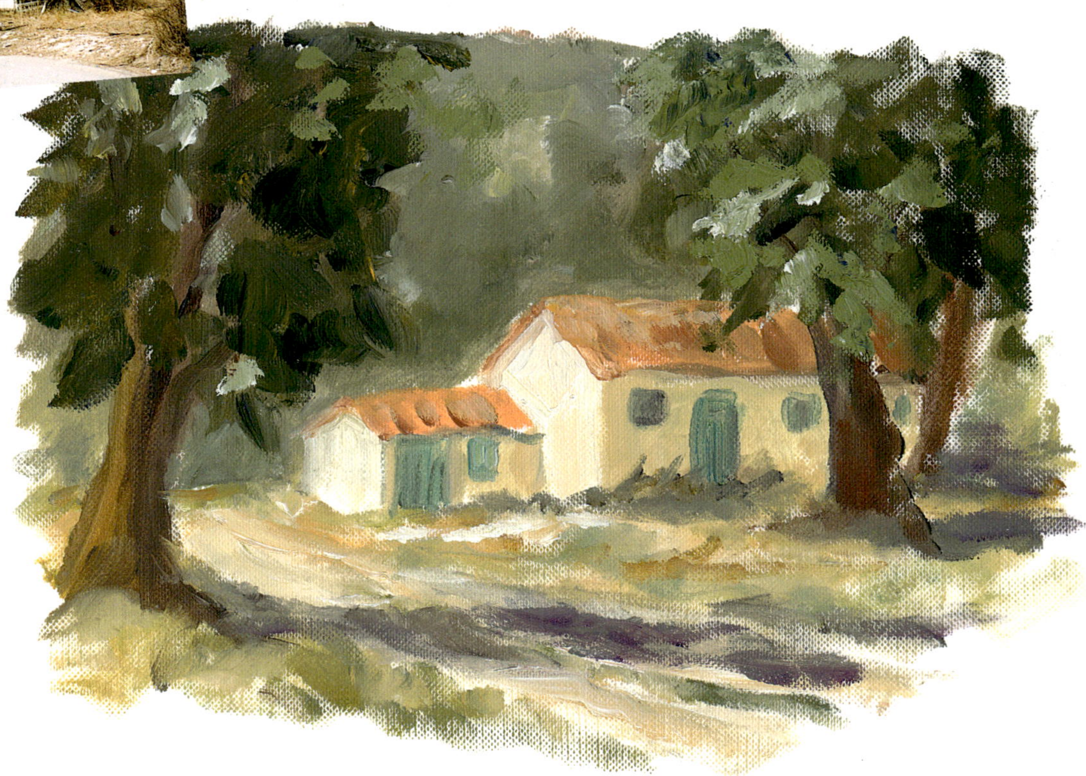

▶ In my colour study for a painting of the hut I exaggerated the difference between the trees in front of the building and the bank of woodland behind it. I also left out the fence at the bottom left of the photograph.

Combining several images

While it is easier to work from just one photograph, I often find myself combining two or even three images. Where you have more than one photograph, start by laying these out in front of you. Next make a quick sketch of the composition you wish to develop. This will help you to visualize more clearly the finished picture you are trying to create. Now you should have all the information you need to start painting.

I have used two photographs here for a painting of the River Loire in France. I was happy with the first image of the river with its railway bridge in the middle distance, but the figures were less than inspiring, so I combined this 'composition photograph' with another image taken in Chablis of a boy fishing, which I felt made a more interesting subject.

General advice

A brief summary of how to use photographs for painting may be helpful. Take several photographs from different angles and try not to slavishly copy one image. Work instead with a selection of photographs and produce a sketch from these. Then use the sketch as the basis for your painting, with the photographs as extra information. This way you should be able to produce interesting and lively paintings that no-one will guess were produced with the aid of a camera.

▼ Young Fisherman
25 x 30 cm (10 x 12 in)
The finished painting was produced by using two photographs, and a bit of artistic inspiration!

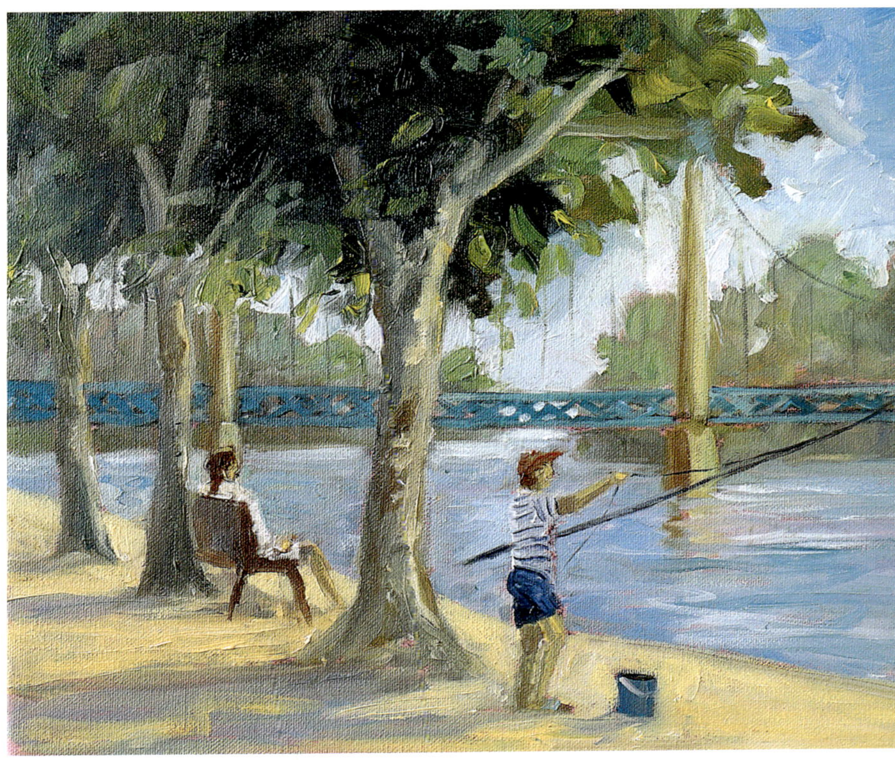

▼ This photograph of a Sunday afternoon on the banks of the Loire was a good image on which to base a composition.

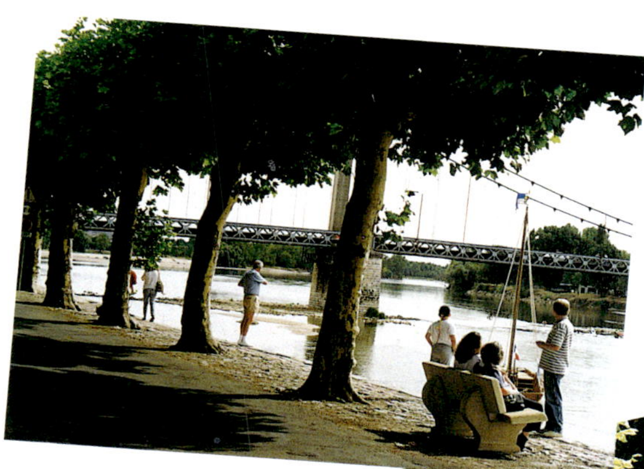

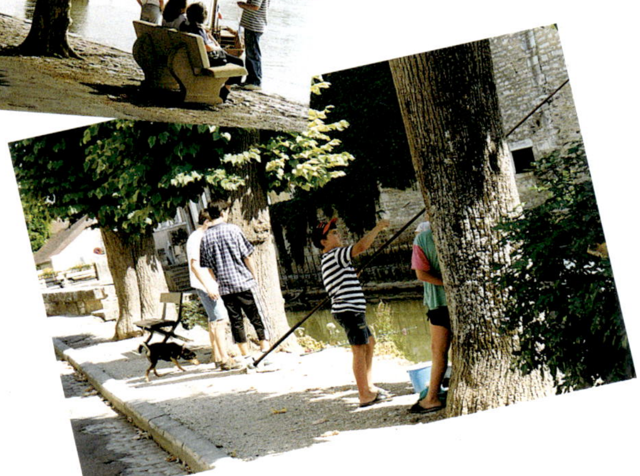

◀ This photograph of a young fisherman in Chablis supplied the detail for my painting.

Atmospheric Skies

Skies set the tone and atmosphere for any landscape, so it is important to be able to paint the sky at different times of day and to capture different cloud patterns. Start by looking carefully at the sky and making a series of quick sketches. It can be surprising just how many colours you will see in the sky, depending upon the weather conditions. I find the most pictorial skies are often those of winter when the sun stays low in the sky all day and therefore is less strong, giving hues that are much more subtle. Even if you do not wish to venture outdoors to paint the sky, simply look out of your window. After all, there is no point in suffering outdoors in the cold if you do not need to. Study the sky as much as you can, making lots of quick oil sketches at different times of the day.

Perspective in skies

There is perspective in the sky as well as the landscape. Place the largest cloud shapes towards the top of the canvas to help them appear closer. Clouds towards the horizon look smaller and tend to be longer. Look also at how the colour of the sky changes from dark blue high up to a cooler pink or turquoise towards the horizon.

▼ I used Coeruleum to capture the open feel of this summer sky. Clouds are white on top with a little Cobalt Violet and Yellow Ochre colour for the shadows.

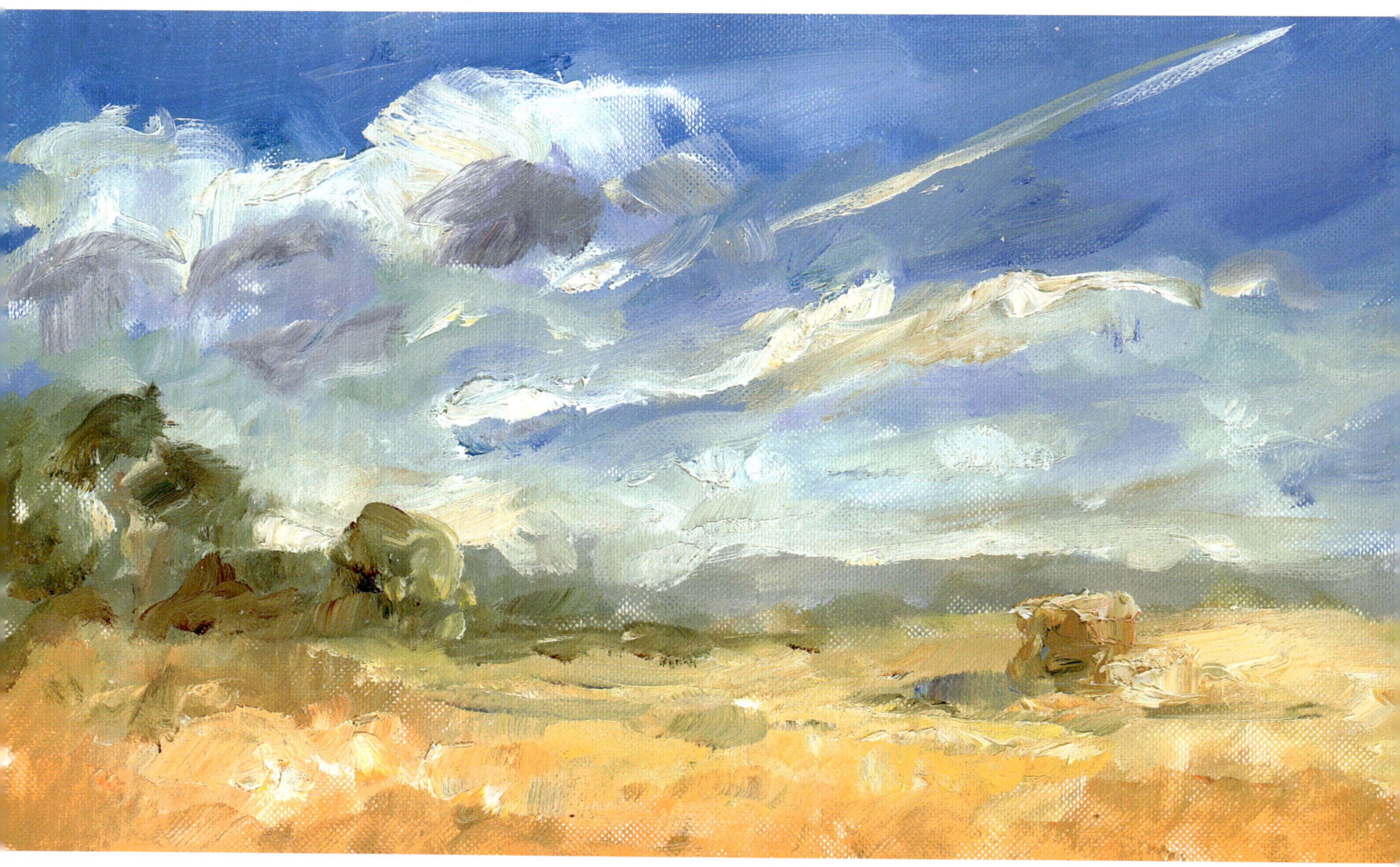

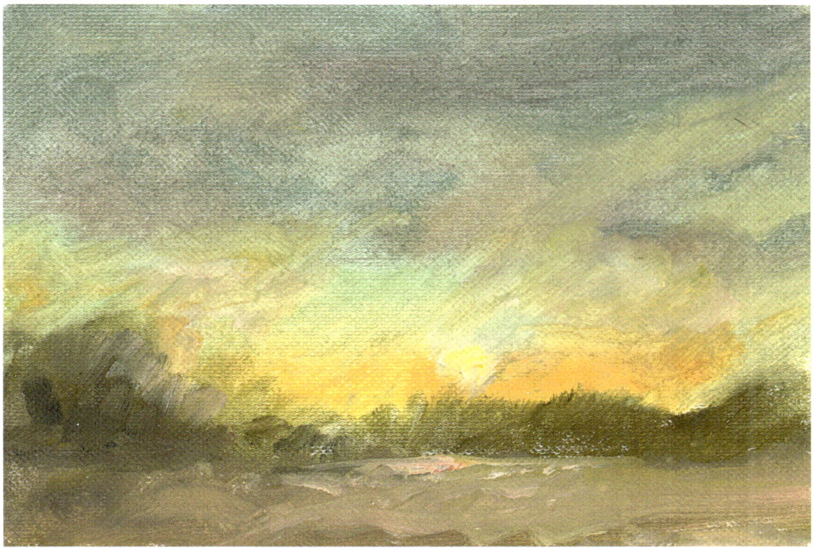

◀ I used Chrome Yellow for the rising sun blended upwards into Coeruleum, making the top of the sky appear a little greenish. Landscape details were kept to a minimum as the sun had not yet risen.

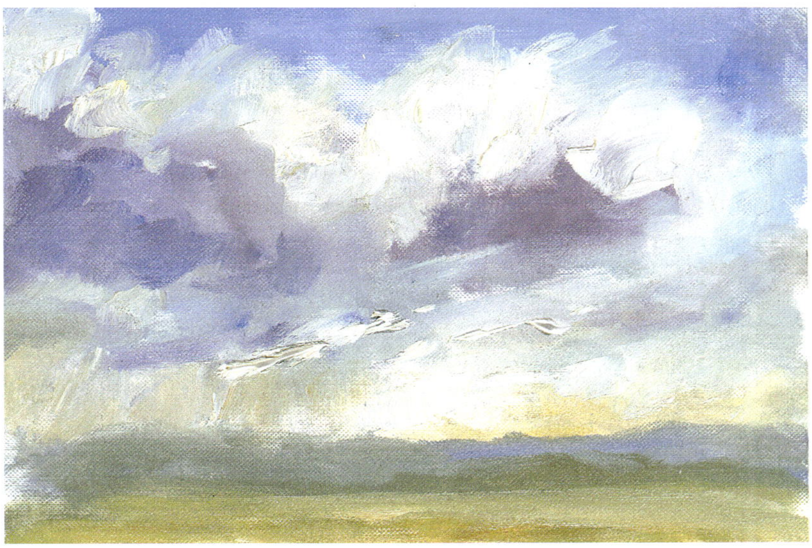

◀ Cobalt Violet, French Ultramarine and Yellow Ochre form the dark base to these storm clouds. Highlights on the tops of the clouds are painted impasto, white with Yellow Ochre. The streaky effect underneath gives the impression of rain falling.

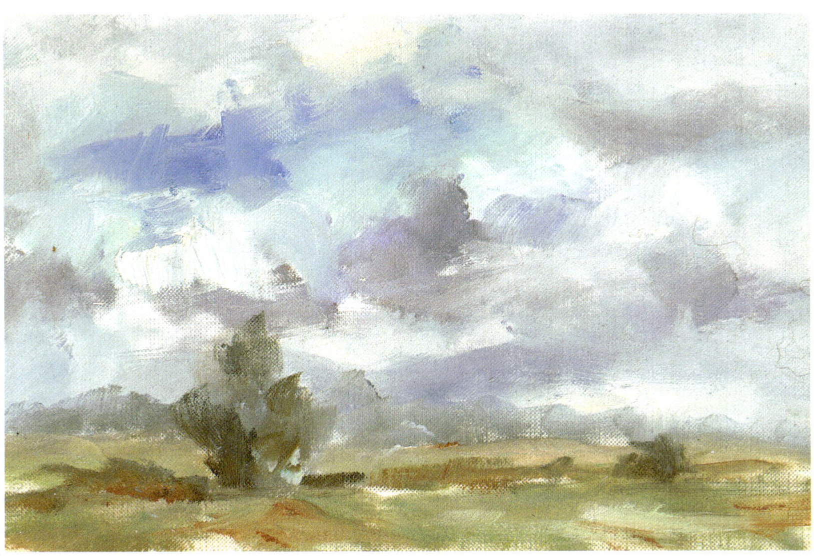

◀ The overall grey of this cloudy sky is a blend of Cobalt Violet, French Ultramarine and white. Varied brushstrokes help to add movement. The patch of blue sky, painted with French Ultramarine and Coeruleum, helps to break up the clouds.

Using coloured grounds

Sky studies can look very effective worked on a coloured background. Warm earth tones such as Yellow Ochre or Raw Sienna have a softening and warming effect on skies, whereas a cooler pink or Vermilion is useful for sunsets. Whenever you choose to paint on a coloured ground it is important to ensure that the surface is completely dry before starting the actual painting. You may find it convenient to use a thin wash of acrylic colour for this base tone as it will dry very quickly, enabling you to get started almost straightaway. Remember, painting acrylic under oil is fine, but you cannot paint oil under acrylic.

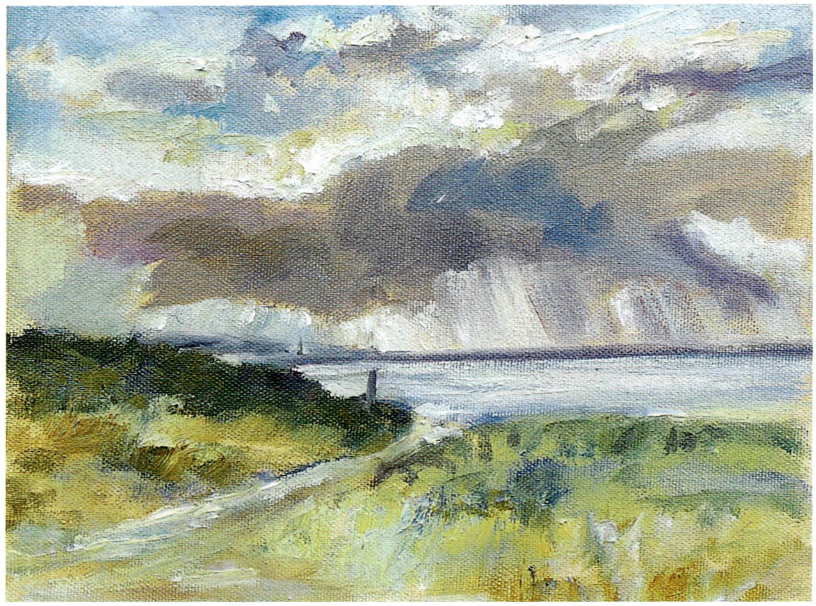

▲ **Towards Evening, Cornwall**
20 x 25 cm (8 x 10 in)
This skyscape was painted as a quick study on a background of Yellow Ochre. Some of the yellow tone shows through the thinly painted cloud shadows, giving them added warmth.

▼ **Ripening Corn**
61 x 76 cm (24 x 30 in)
I tinted the canvas with a thin wash of Vermilion in order to paint these summer clouds. Patches of pink show through, helping to add a light, airy feeling to the sky.

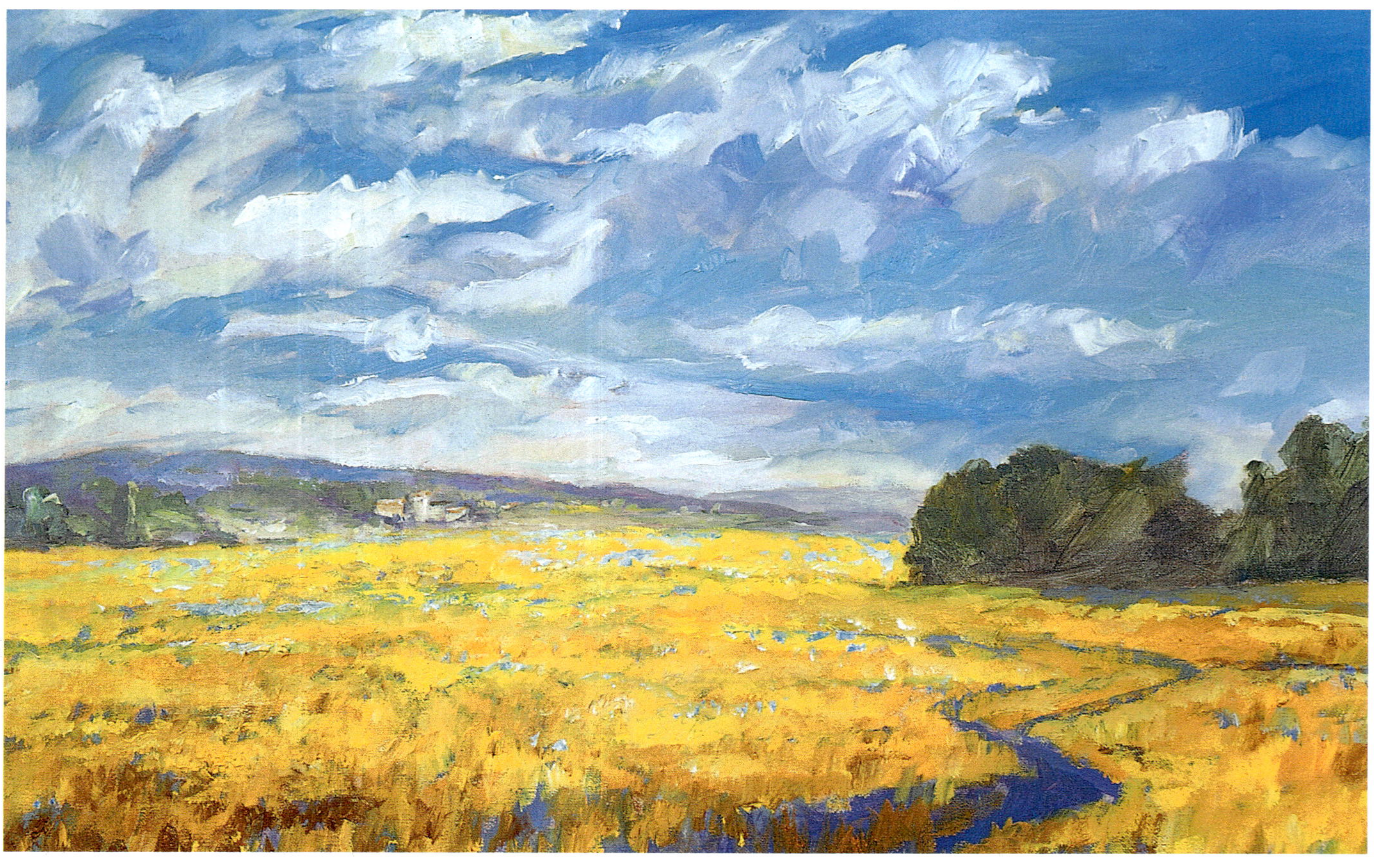

Sunsets

As the sun moves towards the horizon, turning the sky red or gold, it makes a wonderful subject for the artist. However, although the colours may appear vivid in reality, if you paint them in this way, they will look harsh and unreal. If you find that the colours you have chosen are too bright mix up a little scumble glaze using French Ultramarine and white and work this over those areas you wish to tone down.

While you may find it easier to paint a sunset from a good photograph at first, try to do some quick studies from life as well. Keep them small and allow yourself fifteen minutes for each one. These studies will help you to make careful observations and mix up accurate colours at the same time.

▼ I scumbled pale blue over the bottom part of this sunset and the land beneath to tone it down a little, and to lose some of the details and darker tones in the foreground.

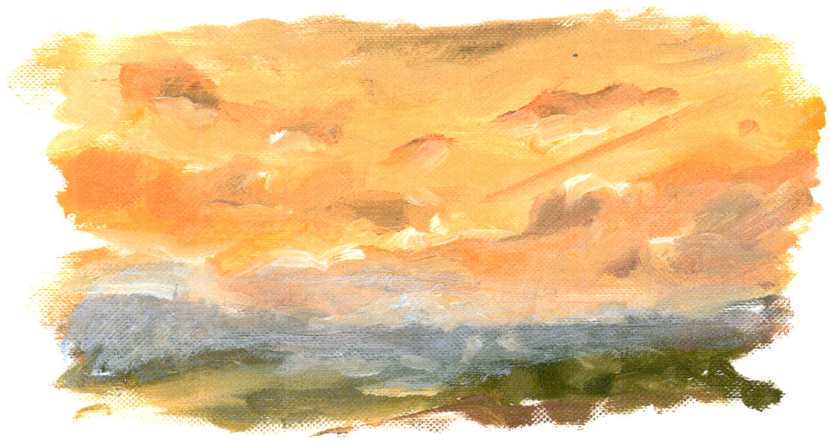

▼ **Towards Dusk, Send Marsh**
20 x 25 cm (8 x 10 in)
The landscape was rapidly losing any sense of detail as the sun sank towards the horizon. I used mainly Cobalt Violet, Naples Yellow and Yellow Ochre for the blend of warm greys and golds in the foreground trees and marsh.

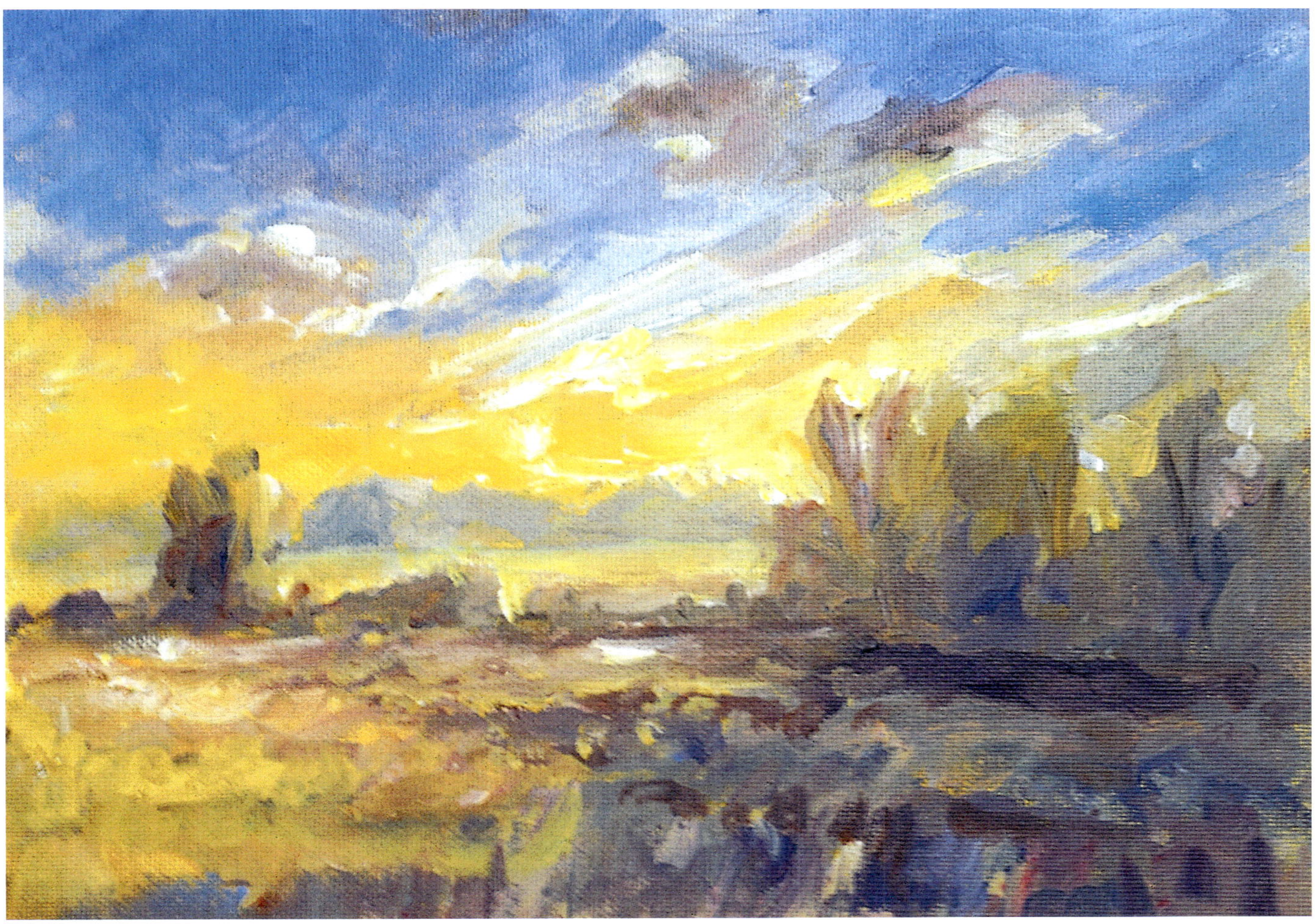

Painting Trees

Trees form an integral part of the landscape, so it is important to be able to paint them well. You do not need an intimate knowledge of every species, but being able to portray the different shapes and characteristics of the main varieties of tree will greatly improve your landscapes.

Each time you go for a walk, take a sketchbook with you and make simple drawings of the trees around you. Concentrate on the overall shape of each variety, noting down the colours of the leaves and main trunk. Building up reference material in this way is very useful when painting back at the studio as well as helping you to develop your eye as an artist.

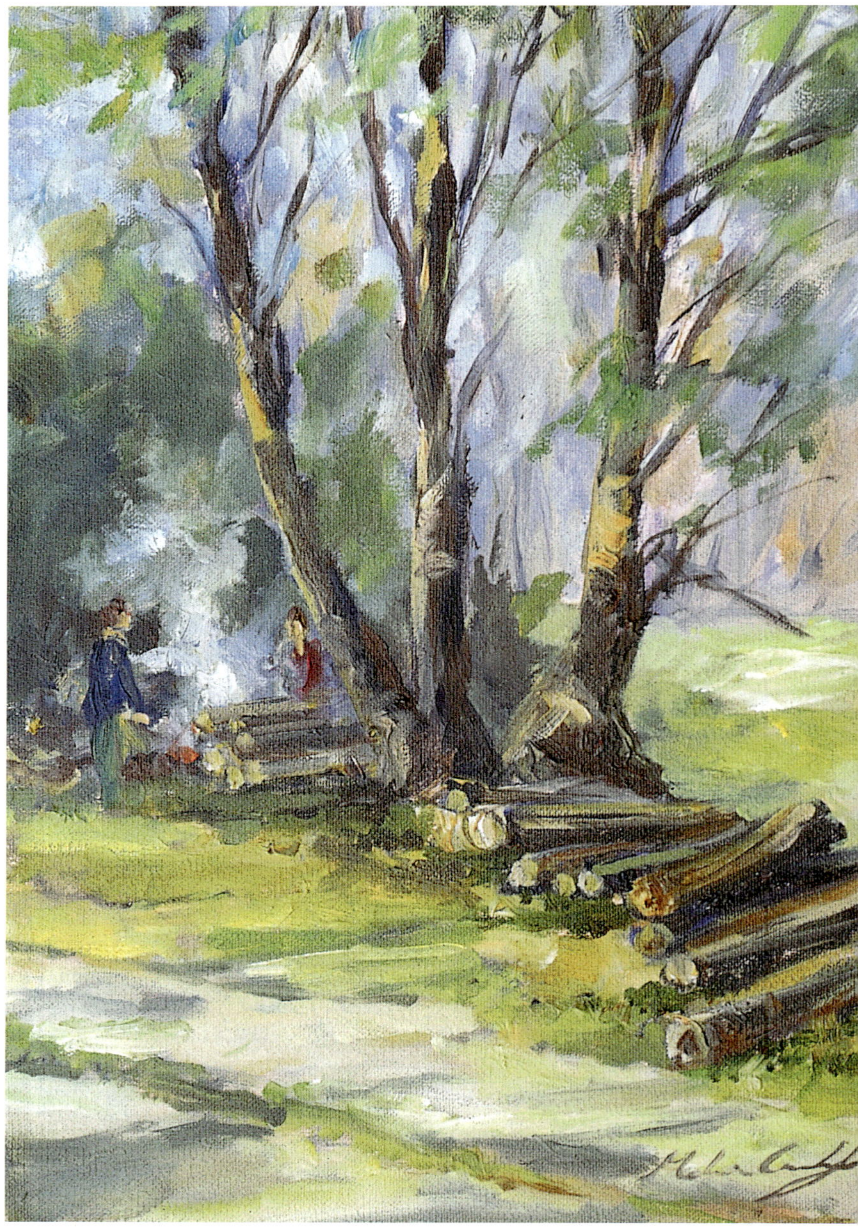

Foreground trees

Even when painting trees in the foreground, try to resist the temptation to paint every leaf. Think instead of patches of colour formed by groups of leaves. See where these catch the light and where they are in shadow. Try to imagine the foliage as a series of abstract patterns with twigs and branches running through. When painting the trunk and main branches, make some of your brushstrokes go across the trunk as well as along the direction of growth.

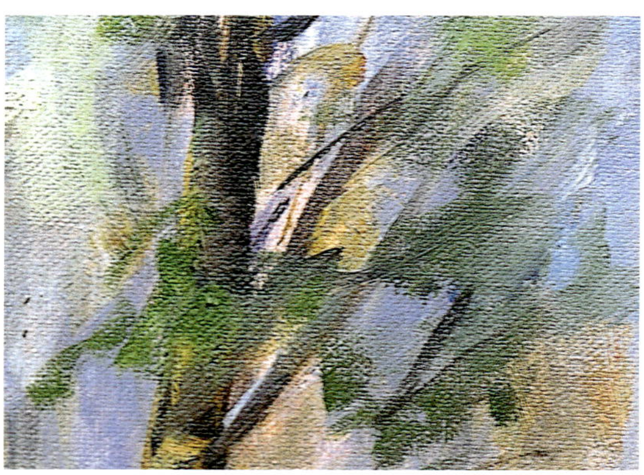

◄ This detail of *Woodcutting at Home* shows how the mass of foliage interwoven with smaller branches is painted to form an abstract pattern of lights and darks.

▲ **Woodcutting at Home**
36 x 28 cm (14 x 11 in)
Note how the foliage has been painted very loosely, even though the trees are the main feature. See how the main trunks go out of the top of the painting, so that they remain in scale.

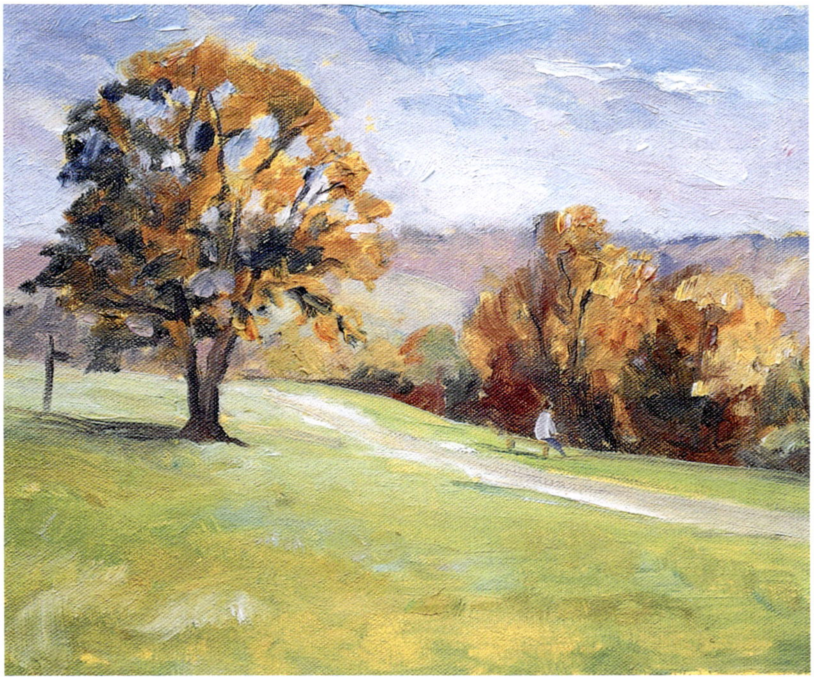

▲ **Autumn Colours, North Downs**
25 x 30 cm (10 x 12 in)
For the tree on the left I first painted the main trunk and branches before adding the foliage. The bank of trees to the right show less detail, with just a few main branches against the foliage.

Brushstrokes across the trunk will help it appear more rounded. Remember, too, to paint in any shadows on the trunk.

Middle-distance trees

For trees in the middle distance, there will be less detail. It is unlikely you can see the smaller branches, so to paint these successfully you need to simplify them. Look first at the shape and colour. Where trees are in groups, treat them as one overall shape rather than trying to paint individual trees. Note where the light catches areas of foliage and where there are shadows. Next ask yourself if you can see any trunks or branches. Only paint those you can see as too much detail may bring these trees too far forward in your painting. Finally, look at the scale in comparison to any foreground trees.

Distant trees

Moving further back into the distance, trees lose most of their details. Even the main trunks may not be visible, so here you will need a slightly different approach, concentrating on the overall shape of the trees. Look carefully at the colour you see and paint this rather than the actual green or gold you know the trees to be. Often these distant trees will appear to be a warm grey or blue-green shade. They may even turn towards a Naples Yellow colour where the light is catching them.

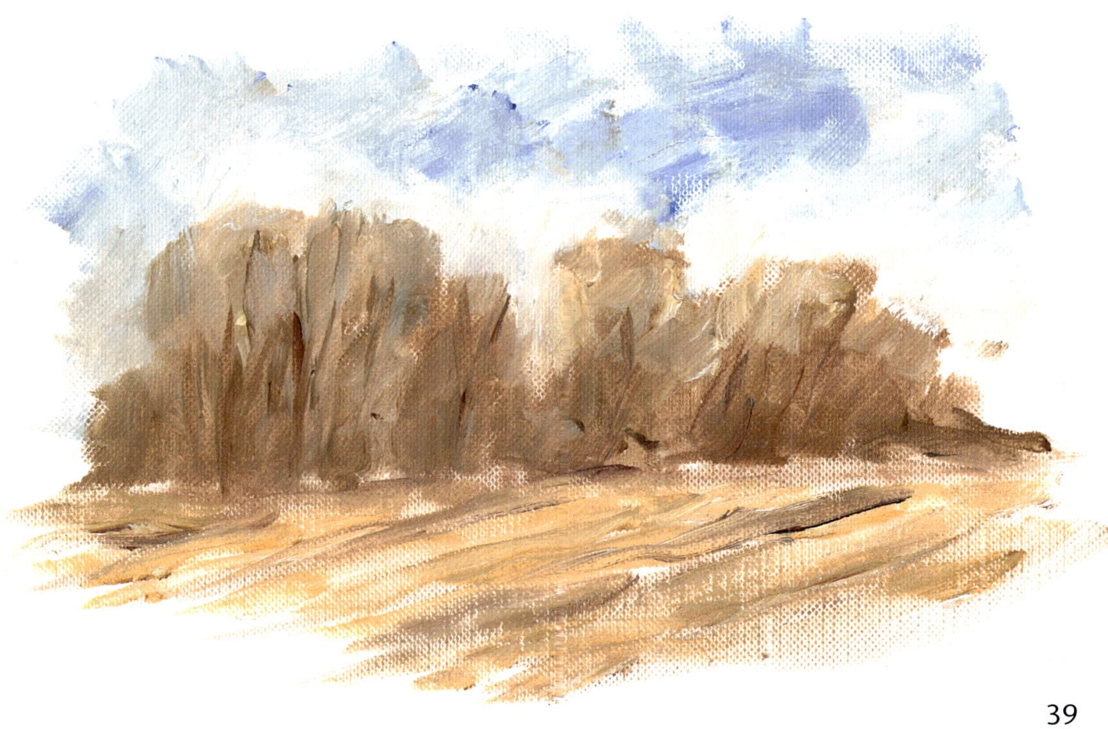

► I used soft grey-browns mixed from Cobalt Violet, Yellow Ochre and white to help the bank of trees recede. I added some highlights with Yellow Ochre and white at the tops, then painted in a few of the main trunks using a darker mix of Cobalt Violet and Yellow Ochre.

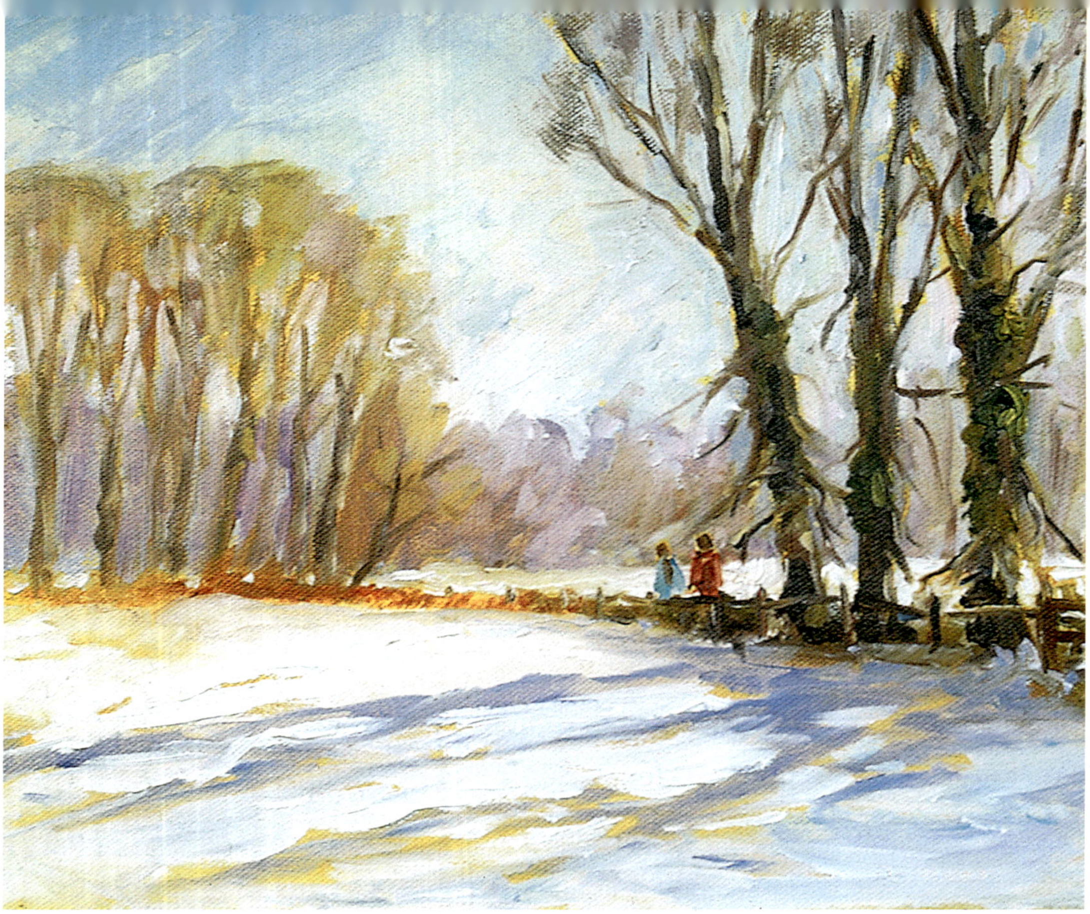

◀ **Sunlight and Snow, Ripley**
25 x 30 cm (10 x 12 in)
Shadows cast by the foreground trees lead the eye into this painting and the focal point of the two walkers. Note how the middle-ground trees are painted with mainly Yellow Ochre and Venetian Red rather than the darker French Ultramarine and Venetian Red of the foreground trees, helping them to sit in the middle distance.

Winter trees

Winter is an excellent time to study trees. Most lose their leaves, enabling you to see the intricate pattern of branches. Depending on the species, branches may be a variety of colours from warm greys and browns to red-oranges or even dark purple. Take time to look around you in winter and enjoy discovering for yourself the wonderful variety of trees in the landscape.

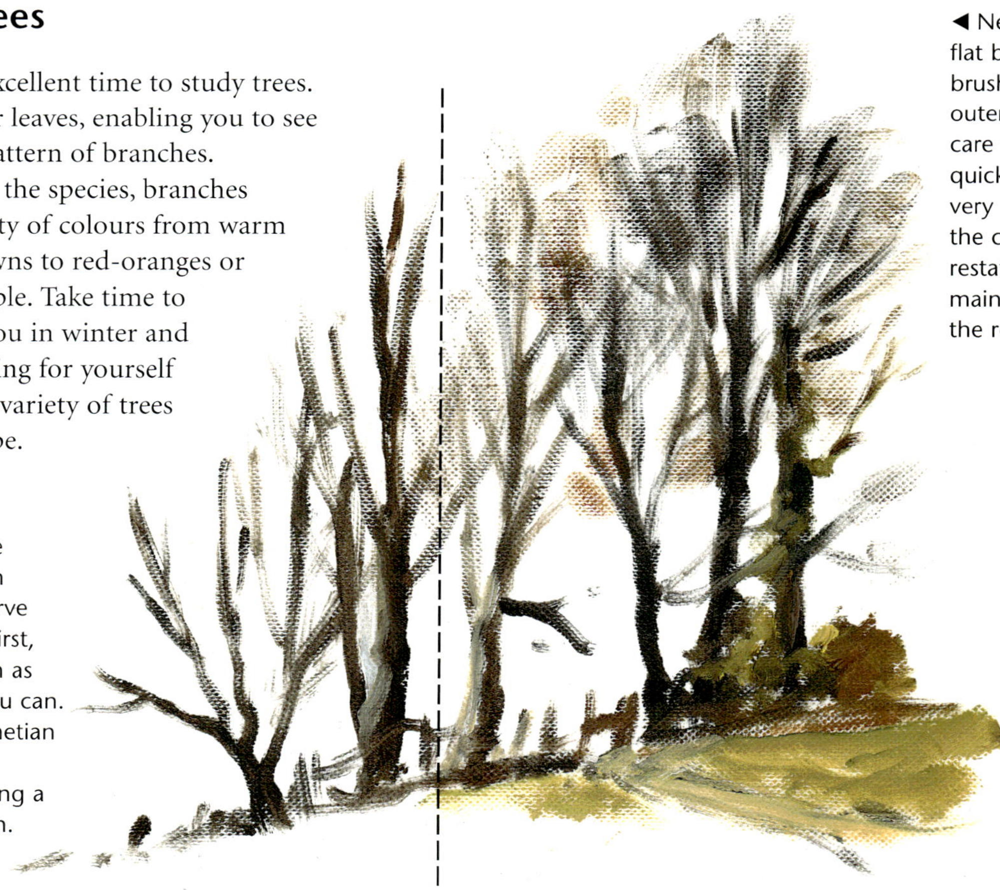

▶ Start with the trunks and main branches. Observe them carefully first, then paint them as accurately as you can. Try a mix of Venetian Red and French Ultramarine, using a fine round brush.

◀ Next use a small flat brush to add dry brushstrokes for the outer foliage. Take care to do this with quick movements and very light pressure on the canvas. Finally, restate some of the main branches using the round brush.

Summer foliage

Painting foliage, whether on one individual tree or within a woodland, requires a similar approach. Draw in the main shape and branches with a soft pencil, then establish where the light is coming from as this will determine the light and darker sides of the tree. I prefer to block in the darker areas of foliage first, usually with a 12 mm (½ in) flat brush and fairly thin paint. This avoids having too much detail at an early stage.

Next you can consider the mid tones and paint these areas with slightly thicker paint. You can then bring the tree together by putting in the trunk and main branches. Dragging a No. 4 round brush into areas of still-wet foliage helps blend the branches into the tree. Put in the highlights on foliage using thick impasto brush marks, before adding any sky holes, also with thick impasto brush marks, delicately applied. Wipe your brush after each mark to avoid disturbing the underlying paint.

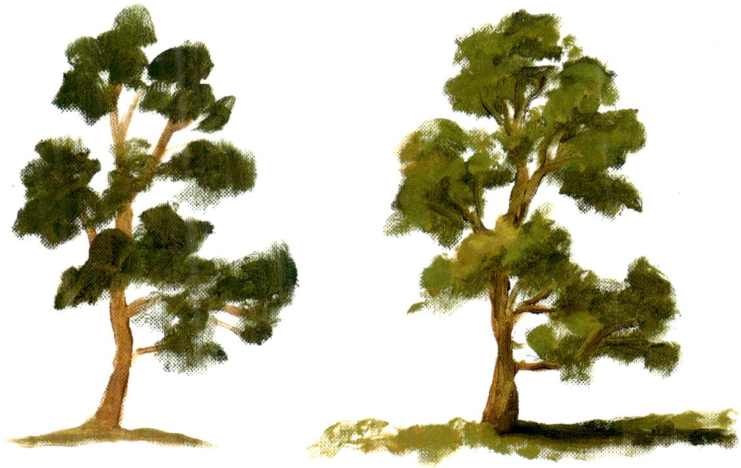

▲ Paint the main trunk and branches. Next, add the darker areas of foliage. Give some form to the foliage by adding highlights to areas that would catch the light. Finally, anchor the tree to the ground with a shadow.

Painting woodland

When painting a woodland scene use the same technique for the foliage, but rather than painting foliage on individual trees try to build up a mass of abstract marks first in the background with soft greens and greys. Then add brighter colours on top. Paint the main tree trunks into the wet mass of brush marks, with those in the foreground going out of the top of the picture.

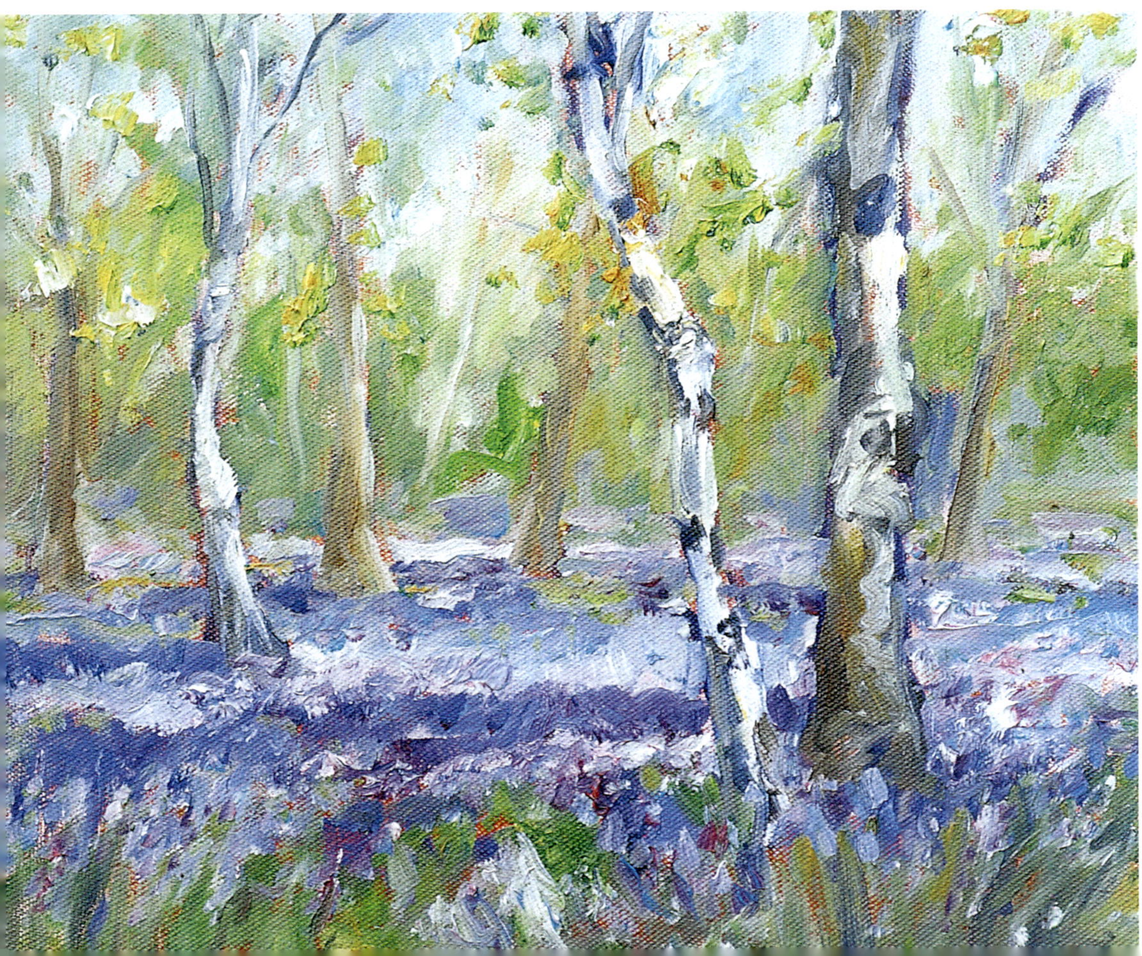

◀ **Kingswood Bluebells**
25 x 30 cm (10 x 12 in)
In order to create depth in this woodland, the colours actually appear darker as they get further away. This is the opposite to more open scenes, but this approach was needed to capture the feeling of looking deeper into the woodland.

Water and Reflections

Water, be it a calm meandering river, the surface of a lake sparkling in sunlight or even puddles down a country lane, always adds interest, light and movement to a landscape. One of the keys to painting water successfully is not to overdo the effect you are trying to create. Take time to observe water in different locations and light conditions. Where there is no movement, reflections can be seen, but as soon as the wind catches the surface of the water these break up into ripples and wavelets and will disappear completely on a really windy day.

There are a number of techniques for painting the different moods of water.

Calm reflections

Reflections in calm water are perhaps the simplest effect to try, but before starting to paint there are a few points to bear in mind.

▼ Autumn Colours, River Wey
20 x 25 cm (8 x 10 in)
Calm reflections in the river were painted using vertical brushstrokes, before adding a few ripples on top with pale blue paint. These were blended softly while the underlying colours were still wet.

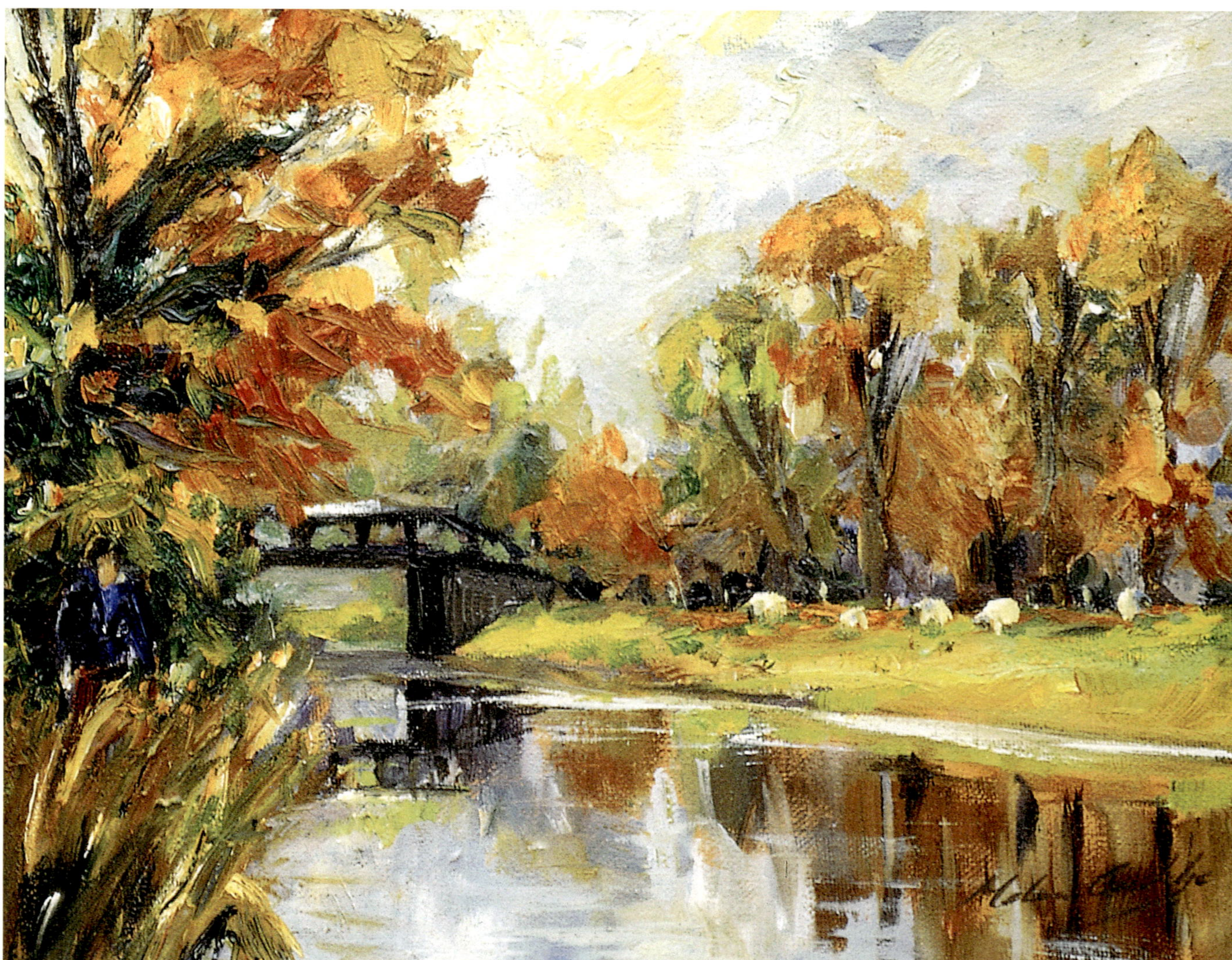

Even in clear water, reflections tend to appear a little darker and duller. If the water is laden with sediment or algae, such as in a canal or pond, then the colours reflected may appear greenish or brownish.

Oils are ideally suited to painting reflections because they remain wet for some time, enabling you to softly blend the reflections before adding any surface ripples. Adding ripples while the underlying colour is still wet allows you to blend the brushstrokes slightly so that they pick up a little of the colour below and sit into the water rather than appearing as lines drawn on top. I find the best way to gently distort the reflected image is to use the sharp edge of a flat 12 mm (½ in) brush.

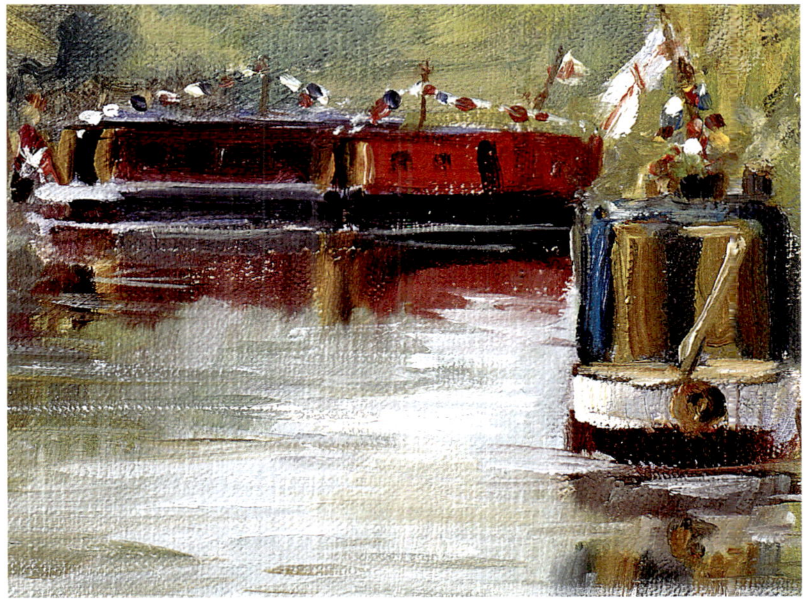

▲ In this detail of *Boat Festival, Guildford* (see page 44) I painted the boat reflections first, in slightly darker tones than for the boats. The water surface was added in pale blue paint, then I gently distorted the reflected image with the edge of a flat brush.

▼ This study shows how to paint reflections in three stages. Start at the left-hand side with the bank of trees and a thin wash of dark green for the water. Next paint in the reflections of the trees. Because the green is still wet, your reflected trees should appear a little darker. Finally, add a few streaks of pale blue for the ripples, using the edge of a 12 mm (½ in) flat brush.

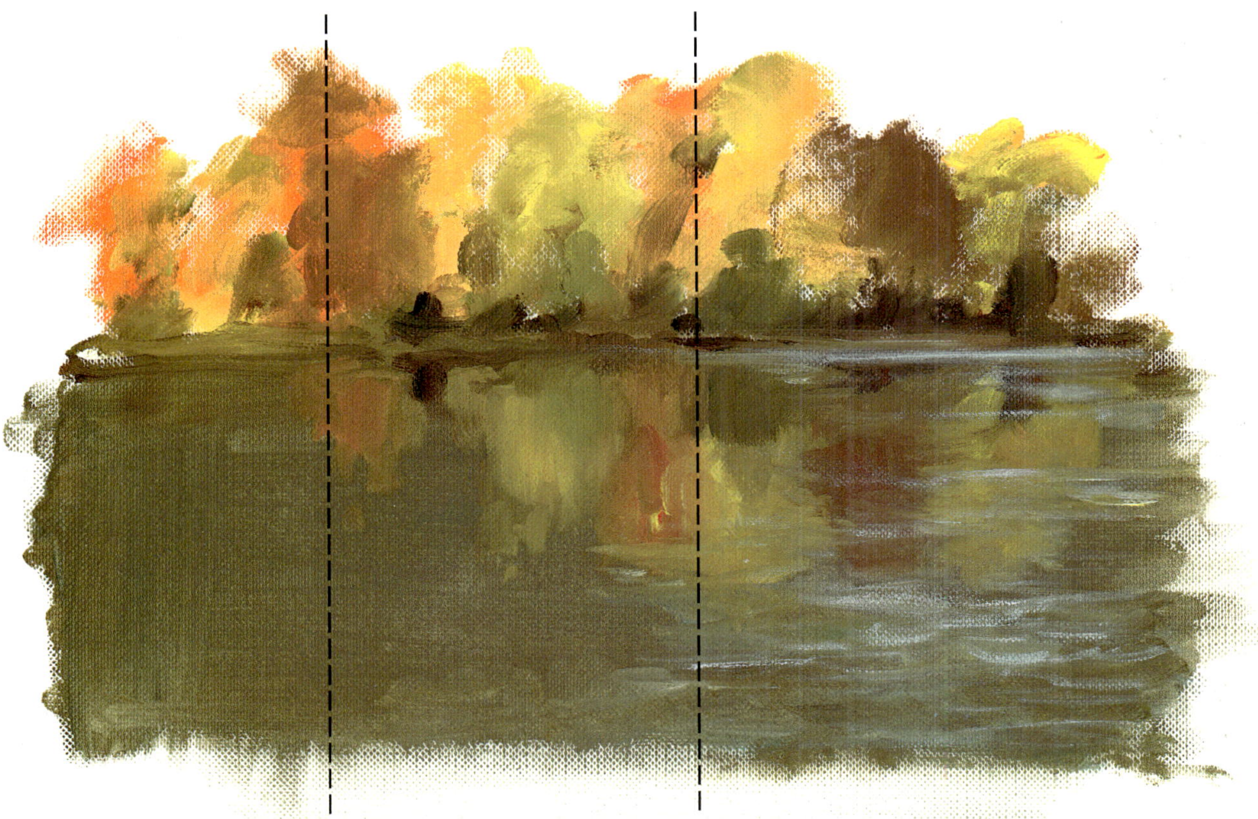

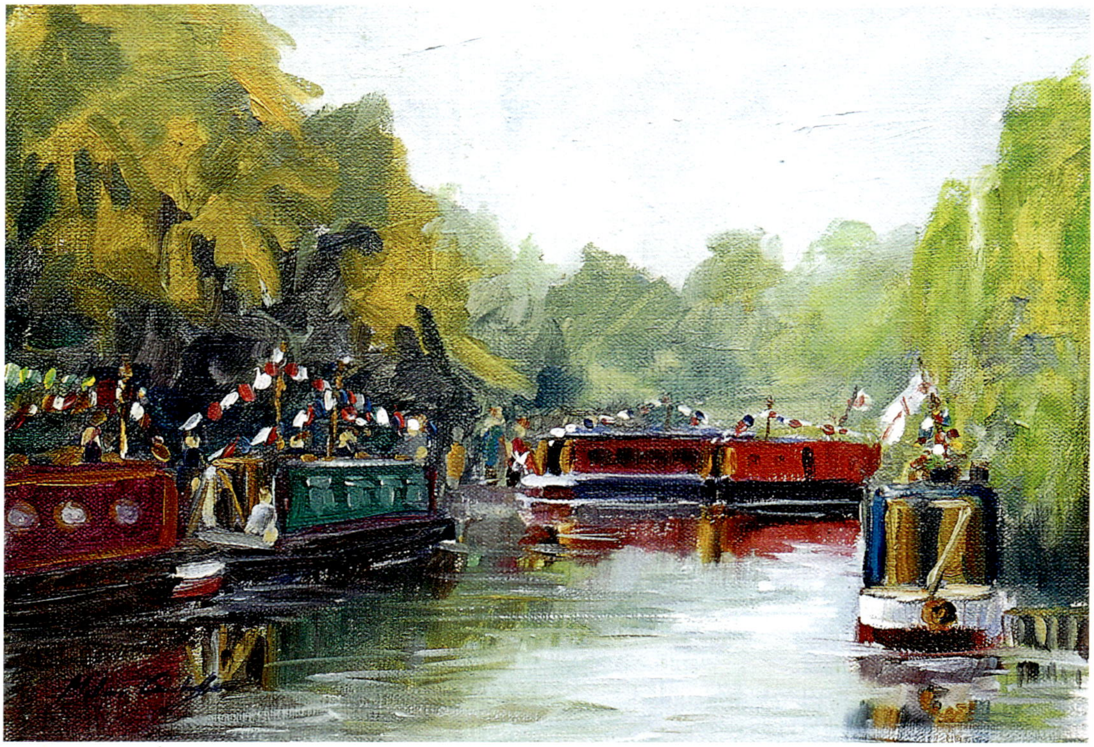

◀ **Boat Festival, Guildford**
30 x 41 cm (12 x 16 in)
The reflections here are distorted, but were painted using the same technique as for still reflections. Then I added more ripples to the water surface, thus breaking up the reflections a little more.

Distorted reflections

Whenever the wind catches the surface of the water, it will create ripples. As the water surface becomes more distorted, so reflections gradually break up until eventually they disappear completely.

When painting these slightly distorted reflections remember that the wind tends to catch the water surface in some places but not others. To make your ripples look more realistic place them in blocks rather than spread across the whole river or lake.

Ripples with no reflections

Where there are no reflections, such as with the open sea, you will need a different approach. Start with a 25 mm (1 in) flat brush and block in the overall colour of the water. Then change to a No. 4 round brush to paint the ripples and wavelets into this wet surface. Ripples can be added as a darker tone of the colour used for the base water, before adding a few highlights to the tops of some of the waves.

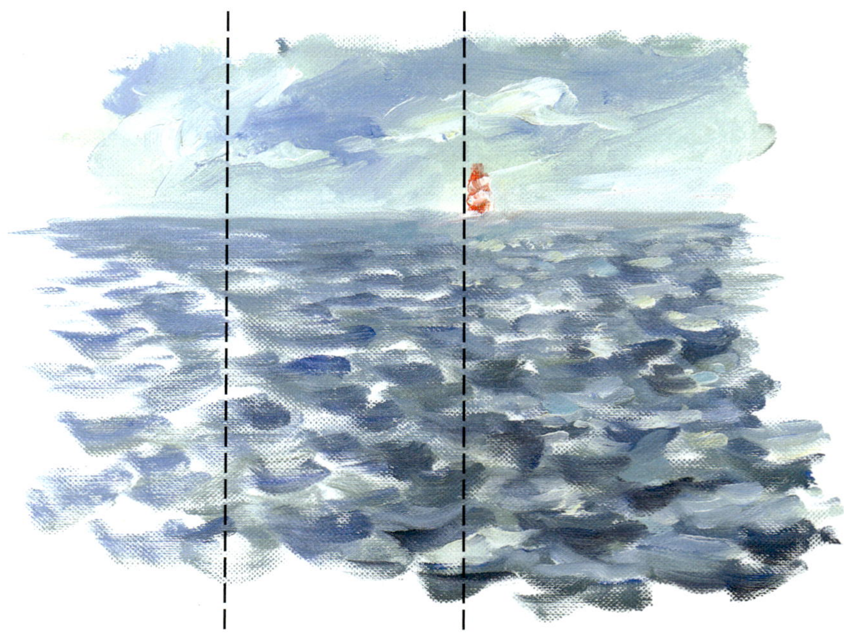

▲ Painting ripples on the sea can be done in three stages. Starting at the left, using a mix of French Ultramarine and white, I painted a series of ripples, remembering to make them larger towards the bottom of the paper. Next I added darker ripples with French Ultramarine and a little Venetian Red. Finally, I gave the tops of the waves a few highlights with white paint.

Swiftly applied thick paint helps to create the illusion of fast-flowing water.

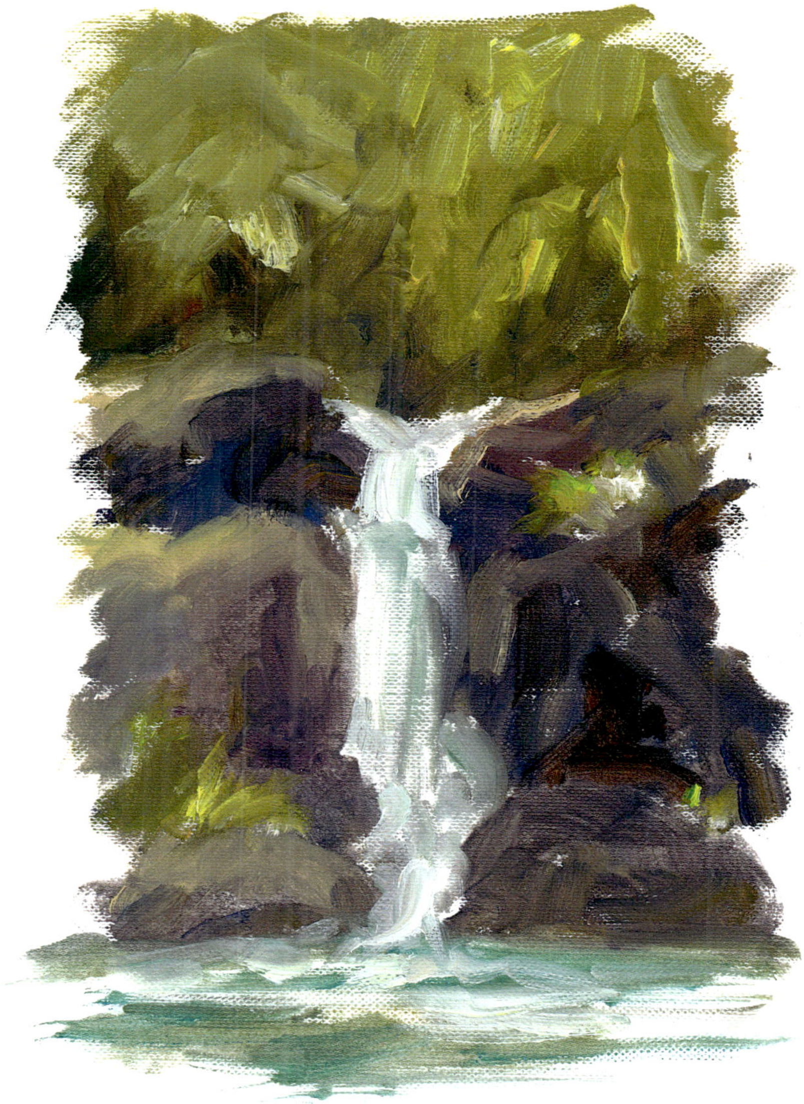

Moving water

Other forms of moving water such as fountains, waterfalls or fast-running streams are more challenging. Although these tend to appear as white streaks of foaming water, you will see subtle contrasts within the falling water. A mix of Coeruleum, Lemon Yellow and white makes an effective colour to use for falling water. Try to ensure you have some dark tones alongside the streak of foaming water as this will help to create movement. This is particularly important when painting a waterfall – the wet rocks would be nearest to the falling water, so this is where your greatest contrast should be.

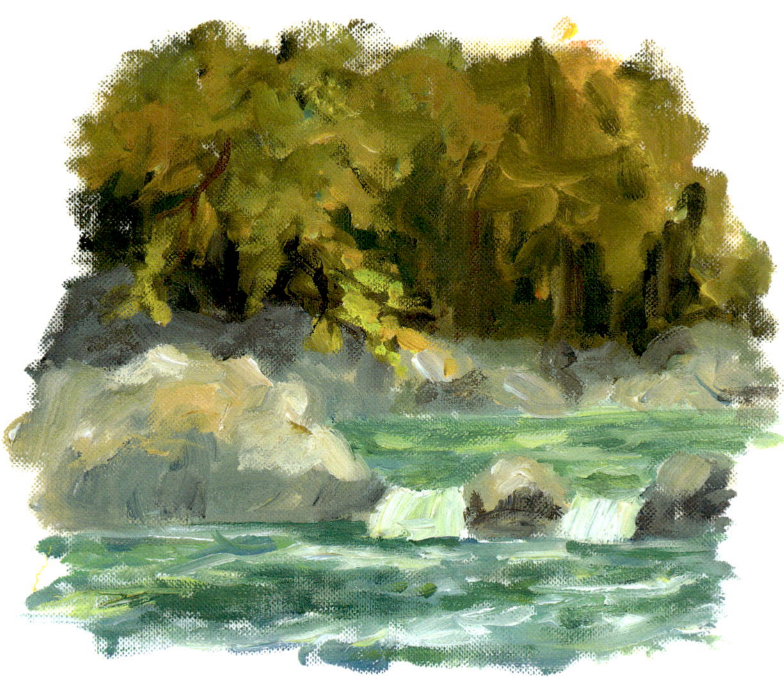

◀ Fast-flowing waters, such as this mountain stream, sometimes appear quite turquoise, so try a mix of Coeruleum, Lemon Yellow and white. The streaks of white water falling between the smaller rocks also help to speed up the flow.

▲ This simple waterfall study uses both the contrast of dark rocks alongside the falling water and streaks of blue-grey within the water itself to add a sense of movement.

Rocks and Mountains

Not all of us are lucky enough to live in the mountains or on a dramatic coastline, but many of us travel to such places. Whenever I find myself in these locations, I am always struck by the amazing range of colours, especially at dawn and dusk, and cannot wait to capture the landscape with my paintbox.

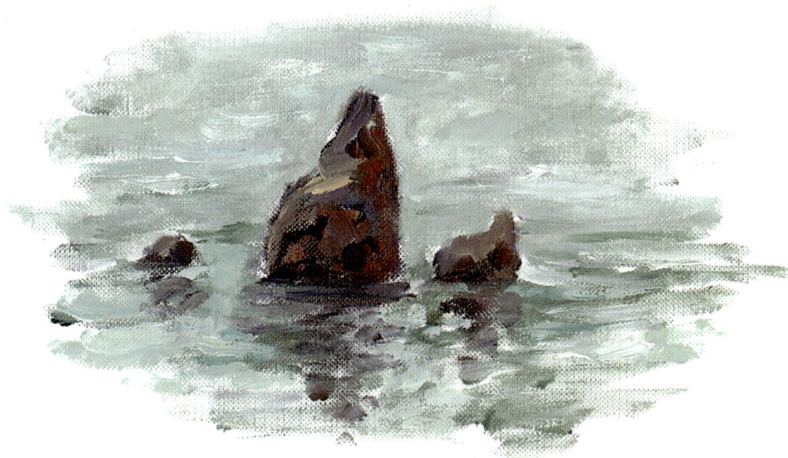

▲ These rocks appeared almost black against the morning sky. I used a 12 mm (½ in) flat brush and a mixture of French Ultramarine and Venetian Red with a little Naples Yellow for the highlights.

Painting rocky textures

In general, rocks and mountains are a fairly easy subject for the beginner. They do not move around in the breeze or change colour as the sky does. Using a flat brush makes it easy to block in large areas of flat stone and details are generally minimal.

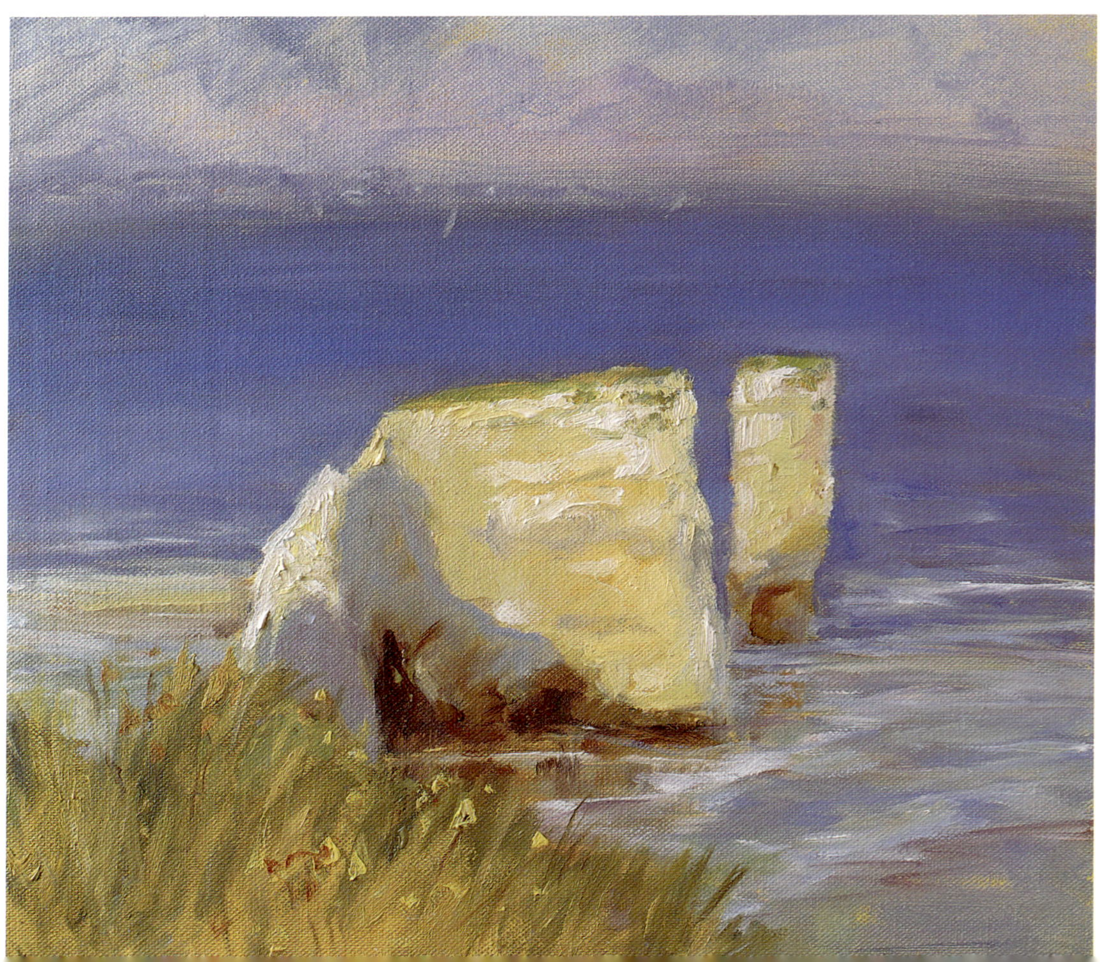

► **Old Harry Rocks**
41 x 41 cm (16 x 16 in)
These chalk rocks may appear pure white at first glance, but look more carefully and you will see they have subtle colours within them as well as the shadow cast by the afternoon sun.

Distant peaks

Unless you are a keen climber you will most probably tend to paint mountains in the distance as part of the backdrop to a landscape. In order for mountains to appear realistic it is important to draw the outline shape as accurately as you can.

Then, look carefully at the colours you see. I was surprised on a recent visit to Spain at just how pink the mountains were, even in the middle of the day. Start by blocking in the main areas of each mountain, adding a darker tone for the valleys and folds. Any details, such as trees on the lower slopes, can be simply rendered as patches and blobs – you are unlikely to see branches and leaves at such a distance.

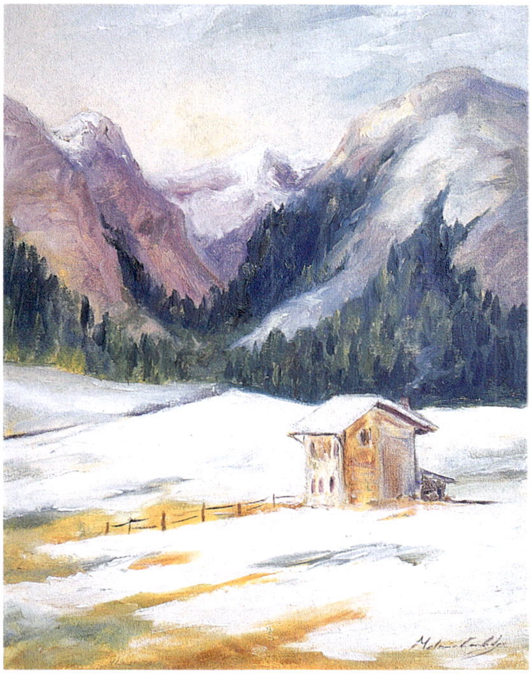

◄ **Spring Thaw, Austria**
41 x 30 cm (16 x 12 in)
The light was very soft for this Alpine view, giving few highlights on the mountains. The sombre mood makes the peaks appear even more dominant.

A sense of scale

When painting such grand subjects as cliffs and mountains, it is important to be able to convey a sense of scale. Including a simple building, bridge or figure can be an effective way to achieve this. Working out what size these should be takes a little care. Whether you are working from life or from a photograph, use basic measuring to get the scale right. If you are including a building check how many times the height of the building would fit into the mountain behind it. You can then easily work out how tall your building should be.

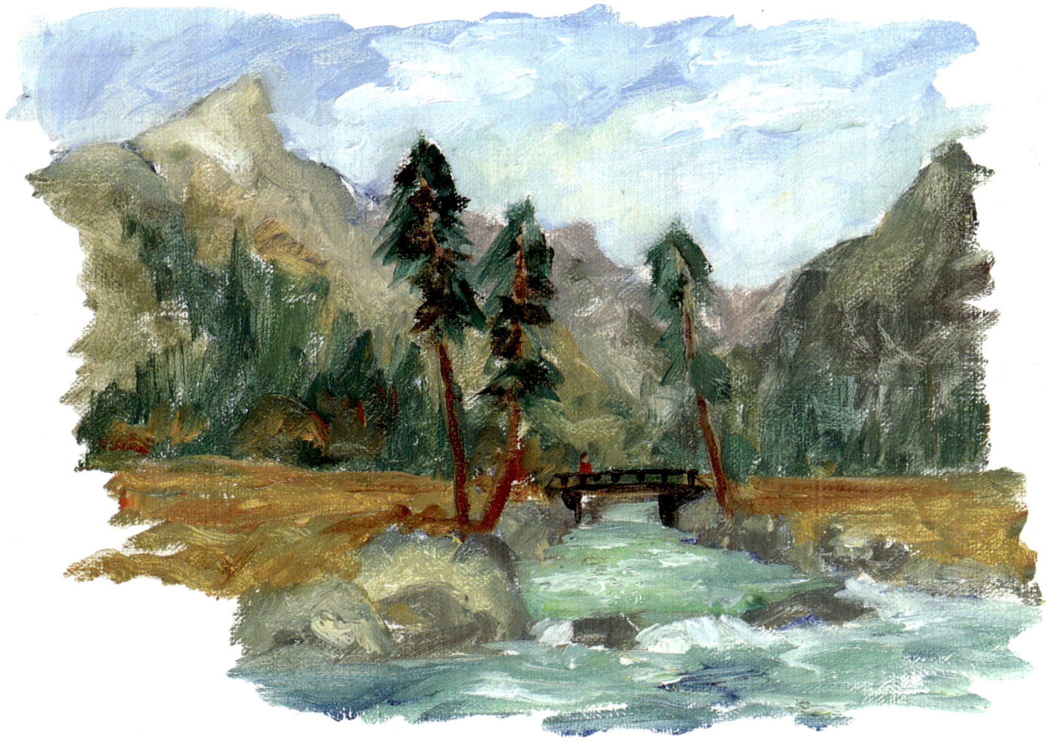

◄ Note just how small my figure is in relation to the distant peaks. Make him too large and all is lost!

Keeping a Sketchbook

Some artists regard accurate drawing as an essential skill, but not all of us are good at drawing. However, it is helpful for every artist to learn to make sketches of some kind. Sketching will help to develop your eye as an artist and over time you will build up a mass of information that will be much more useful than having to rely on only photographic reference material. Do not worry if what you draw seems rough and unfinished – that is how it should be! Simply scribble away, and note down any details or colours alongside. Treat your sketchbooks as a means of gathering information rather than collections of drawings – they will become much more valuable to you in this way.

Get into the habit of sketching. Try to carry a small sketchbook with you all the time; mine is only 15 x 10 cm (6 x 4 in) and this, together with my sketching pen, is always in my handbag or coat pocket. By using such a small book, you can work unobtrusively and quickly. I have even made quick 'people sketches' when sitting on the train as well as in my local pub!

▼ Sketchbook pages showing separate figure studies alongside a drawing of a London alleyway.

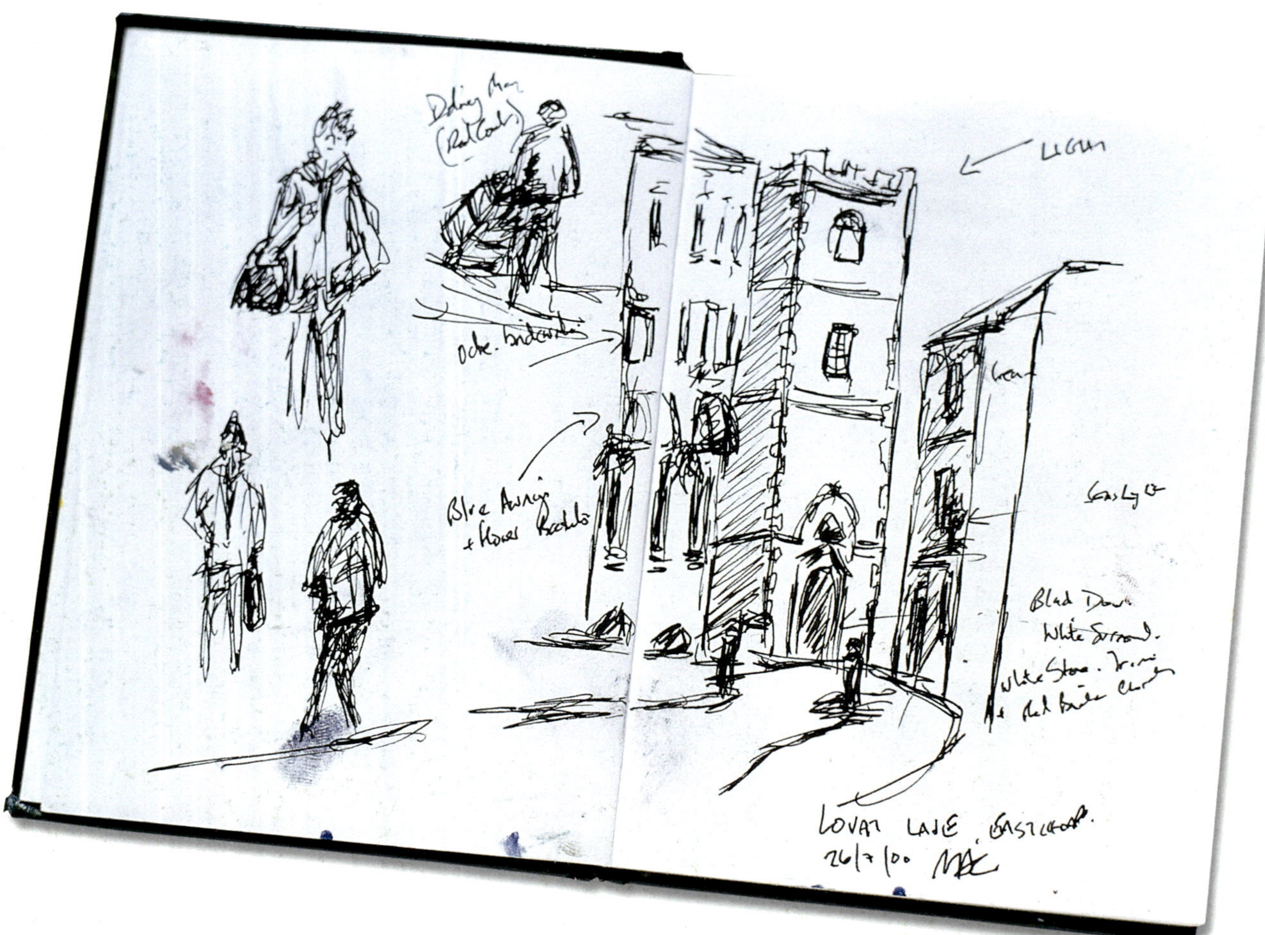

▶ This quick sketch of sheep grazing was made without any drawing at all. Having only my pochade box and no pencil, I simply worked directly with a 12 mm (½ in) flat brush to try to capture in paint the colour and texture on the sheep.

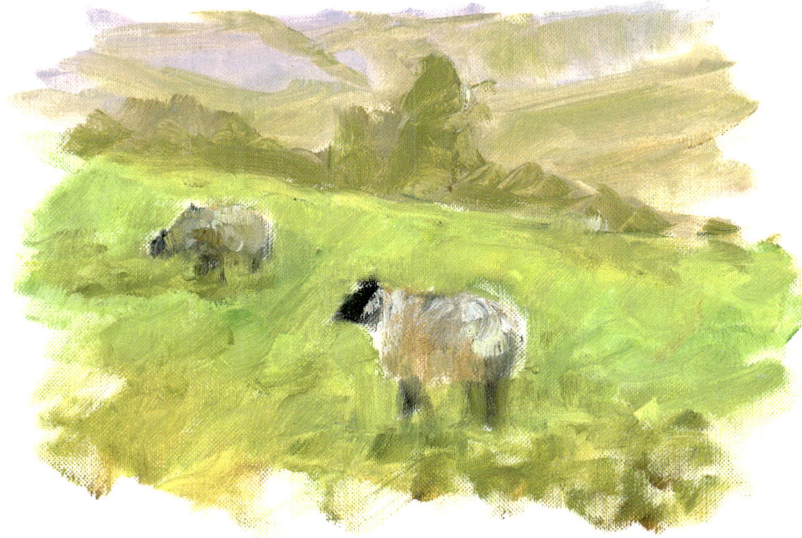

Colour sketches

Sketches need not always be pen or pencil drawings. If you have time, then coloured studies are worth their weight in gold when you get back to the studio. So take your oil paints with you whenever you can; a pochade box is ideal for working such small-scale studies as it holds paints, brushes, palette and canvas boards. Small offcuts of primed hardboard are ideal for these quick colour sketches. Remember, too, that you need only take a jar of alkyd medium with a couple of rags to wipe your brush while working; proper cleaning of brushes can easily wait until the evening without harm to them. Working in this way will enable you to paint anywhere without the difficulties of carrying white spirit or other flammable cleaning fluids.

▼ This rapid oil sketch was made at the beach in north Cornwall. It was a cold November day, so I had to work quickly to keep warm.

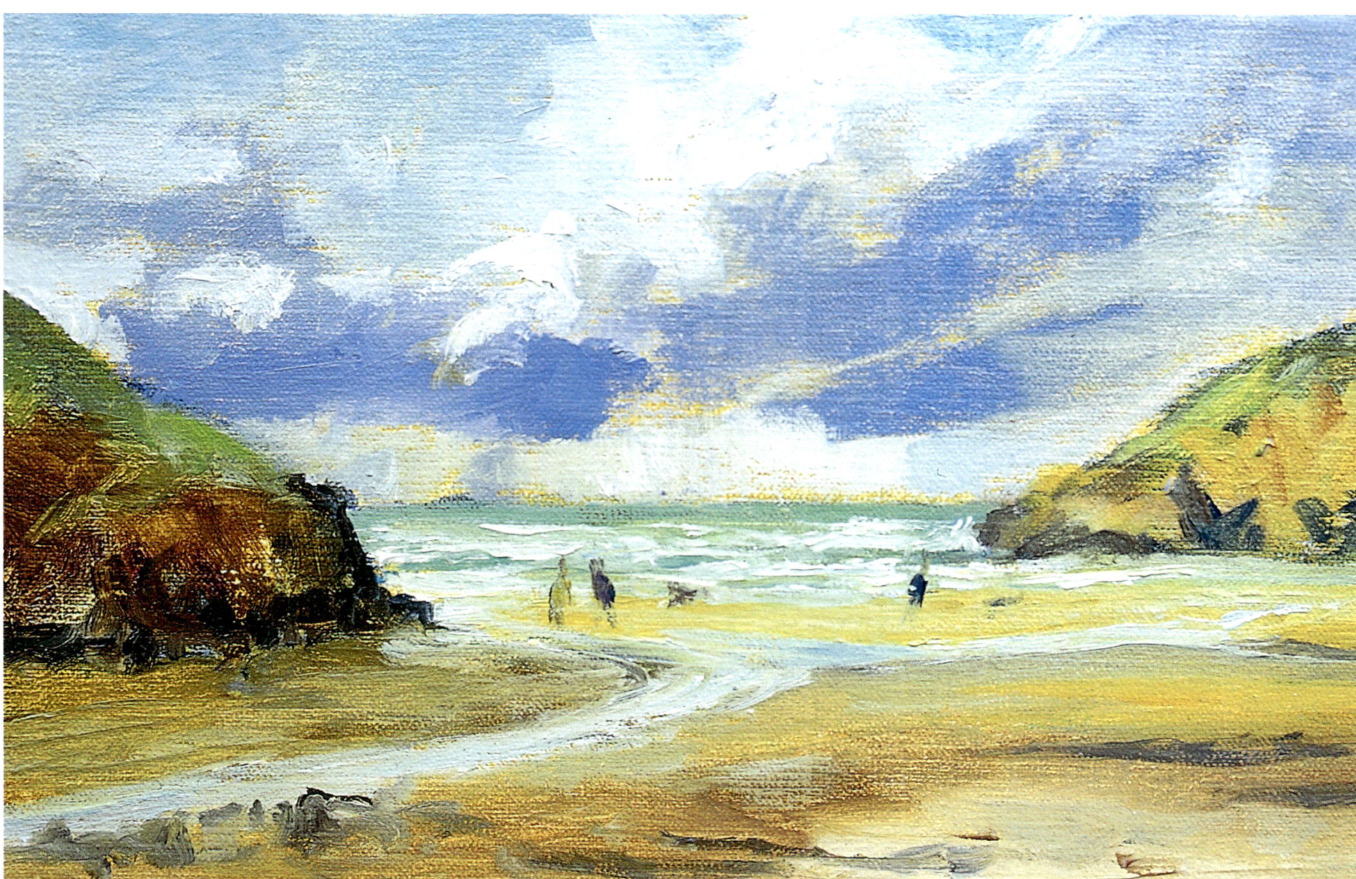

DEMONSTRATION ONE

River Meadows

I love painting the English landscape, especially in summer when there is a wide range of warm greens and softer golds. This quiet bend in the river, with its calm reflections, made an irresistible subject. I painted the scene in the late afternoon when the clouds were beginning to build up. Cobalt Blue helped to capture the summer clouds.

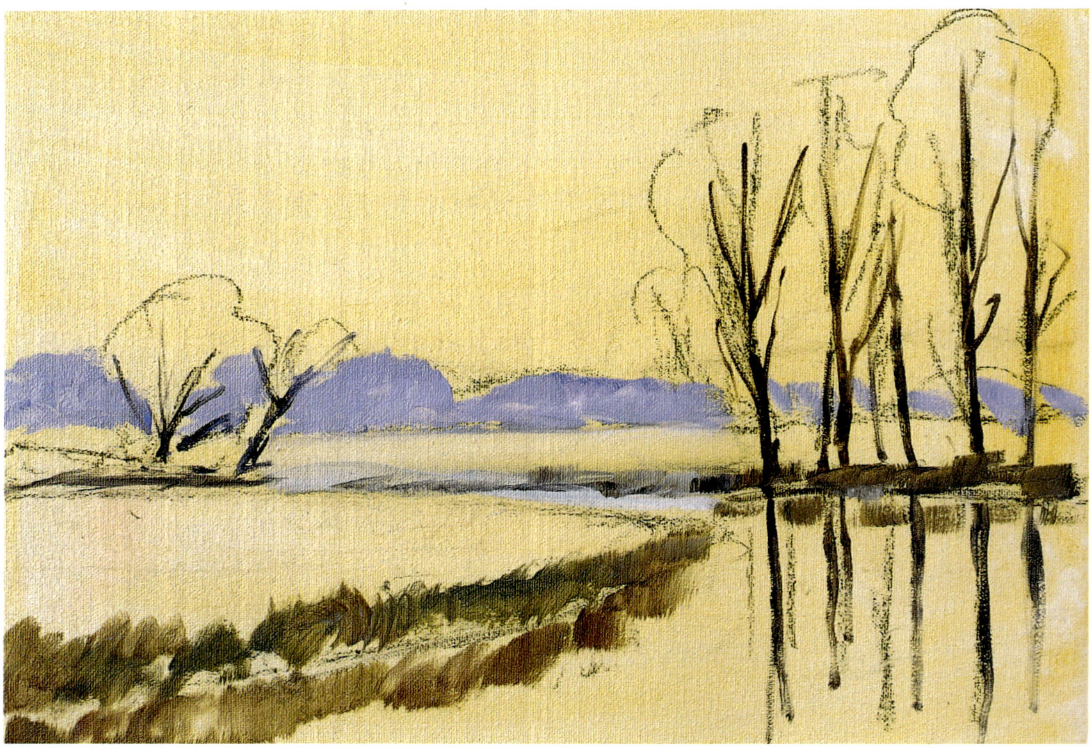

▲ First stage

Colours

First Stage

First I primed the canvas with a thin wash of Yellow Ochre acrylic and allowed this to dry before sketching in the main elements with charcoal. The warm yellow undertone would give an underlying glow to the finished painting. Using a 12 mm (½ in) flat brush and a mixture of Rose Madder, French Ultramarine and Titanium White, I loosely blocked in the distant trees. Then I used Venetian Red and French Ultramarine thinned with alkyd medium to draw in the foreground trees and riverbank, adding the reflections at the same time.

Second Stage

In order to keep my colours clean and vibrant, I painted the foliage of the main trees onto the dry unpainted canvas. I used Yellow Ochre and French Ultramarine for

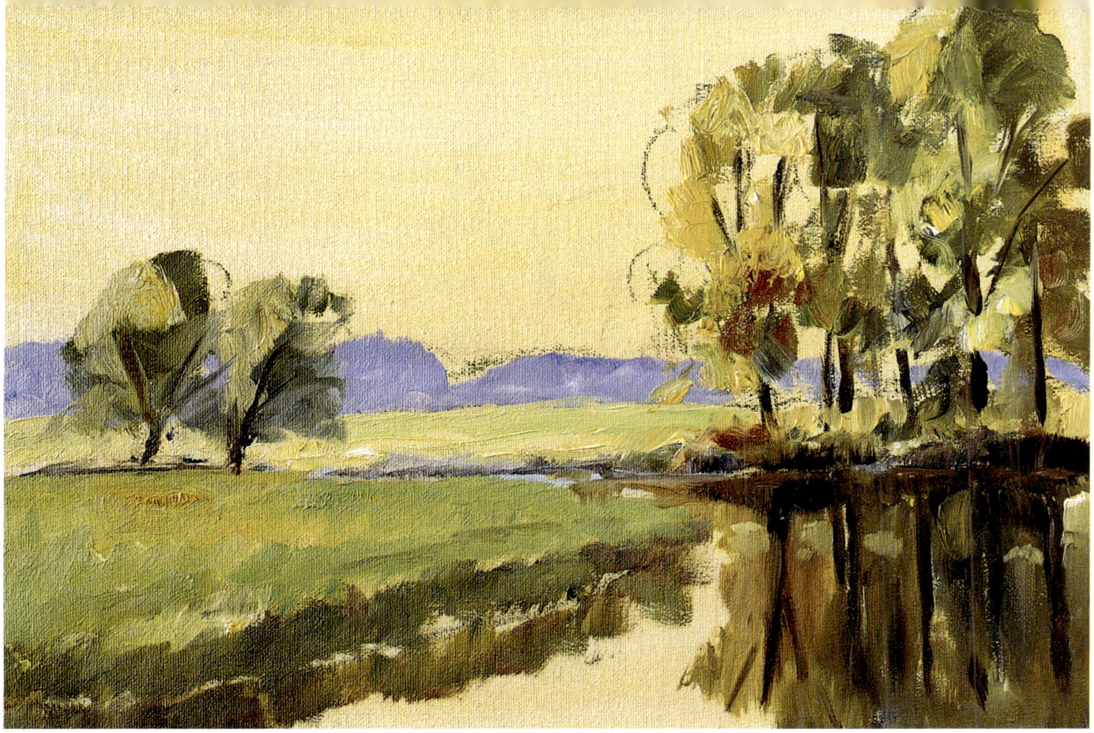

◀ Second stage

the shadows, with Lemon Yellow and Coeruleum for the highlights. Next, using the same colours but adding alkyd medium to help the paint flow, I put in the reflections with smooth downward brushstrokes. The meadow was blocked in using Yellow Ochre and Titanium White for the distant fields, changing to Yellow Ochre and Coeruleum for the foreground.

Third Stage

To paint the sky I started at the top with Cobalt Blue and Titanium White, adding Rose Madder and Naples Yellow towards the horizon. For the sky 'holes' in the trees I used thick paint, which I applied very gently, wiping my brush each time I picked up any green from the foliage. This gave a lively and interesting pattern of light and shade.

▶ Third stage

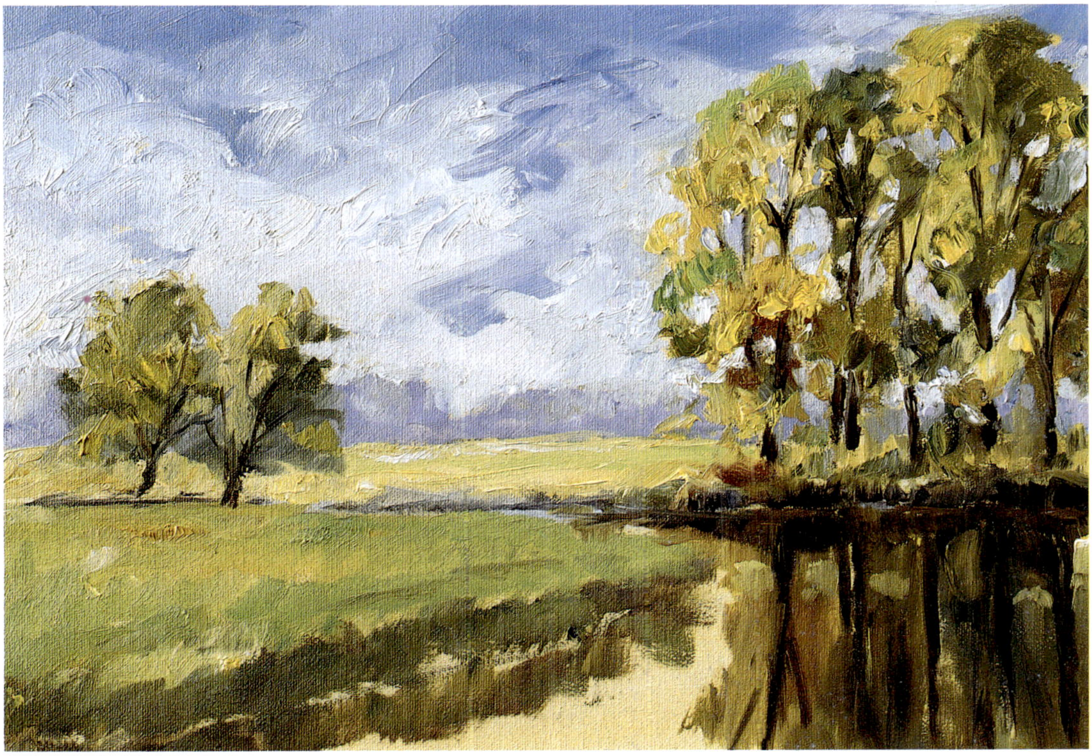

Finished Stage

I painted the water using the same sky colours thinned with alkyd medium, applying them with soft downward brushstrokes to give a mirror-like finish. To suggest the rippled surface, I used the sharp edge of the 12 mm (½ in) brush and a little pale blue (Coeruleum and Titanium White). Finally, I added a few fine branches to the main trees with the No. 4 round brush and a little dark brown mixed from Venetian Red and French Ultramarine.

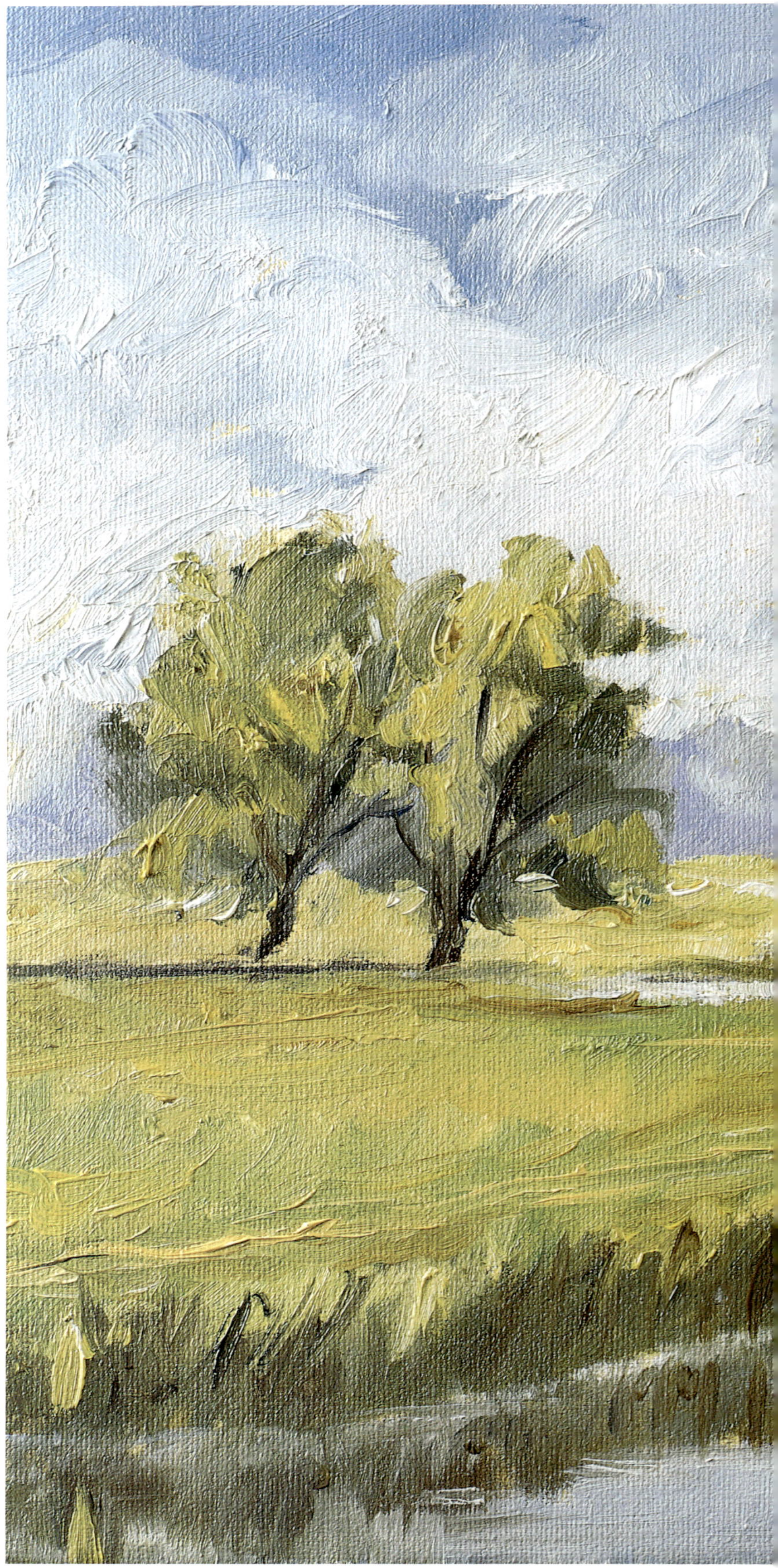

▶ **River Meadows**
10 x 14 cm (25 x 35 in)

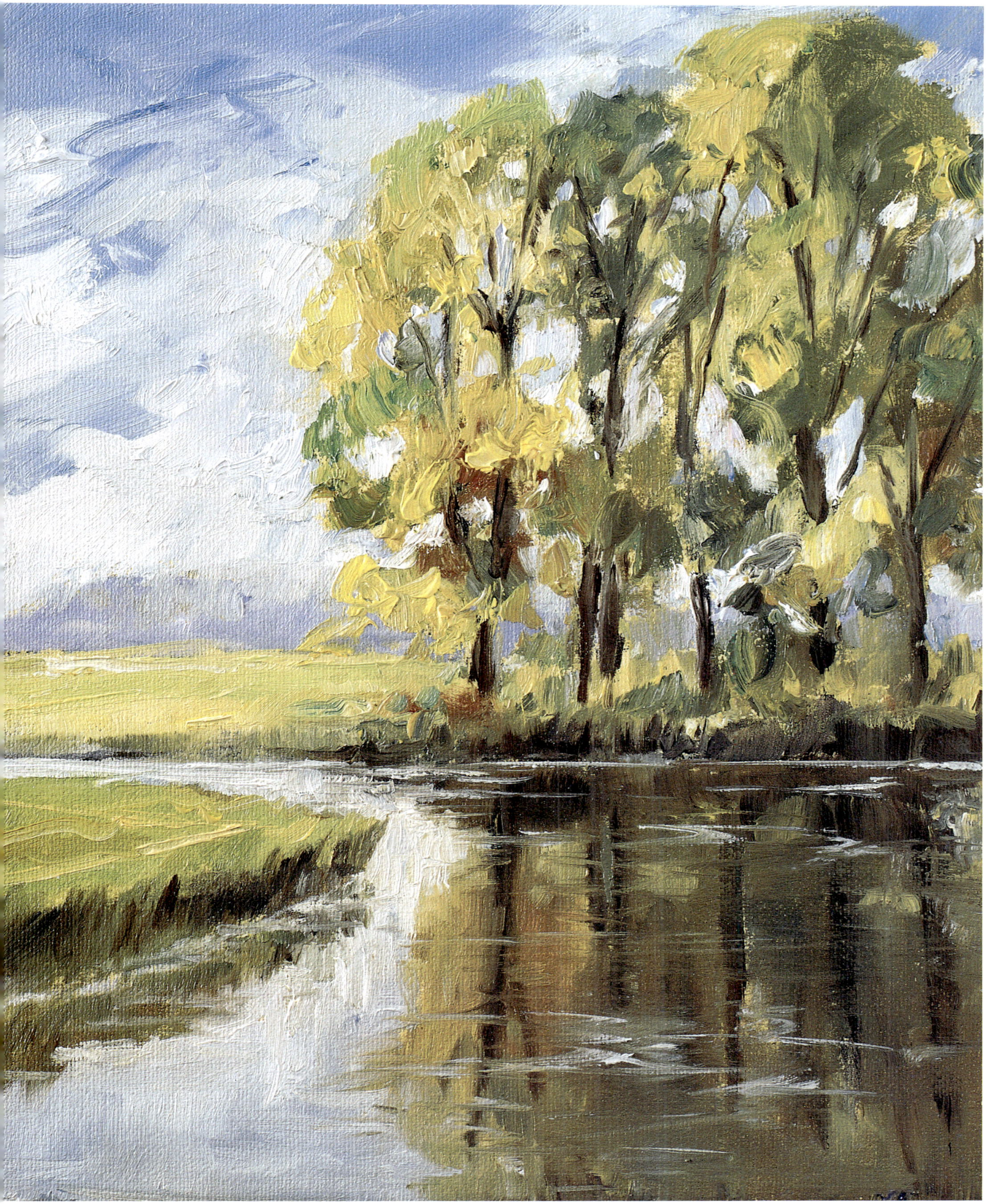

DEMONSTRATION TWO

Alpine View

Mountains make an imposing subject and can seem a little challenging at first. By limiting my palette for this study and concentrating on the different tones rather than too much colour I was able to simplify the subject, yet keep the sense of scale and mass. The ski tracks and mountain hut add human interest, avoiding a scene that looks too desolate.

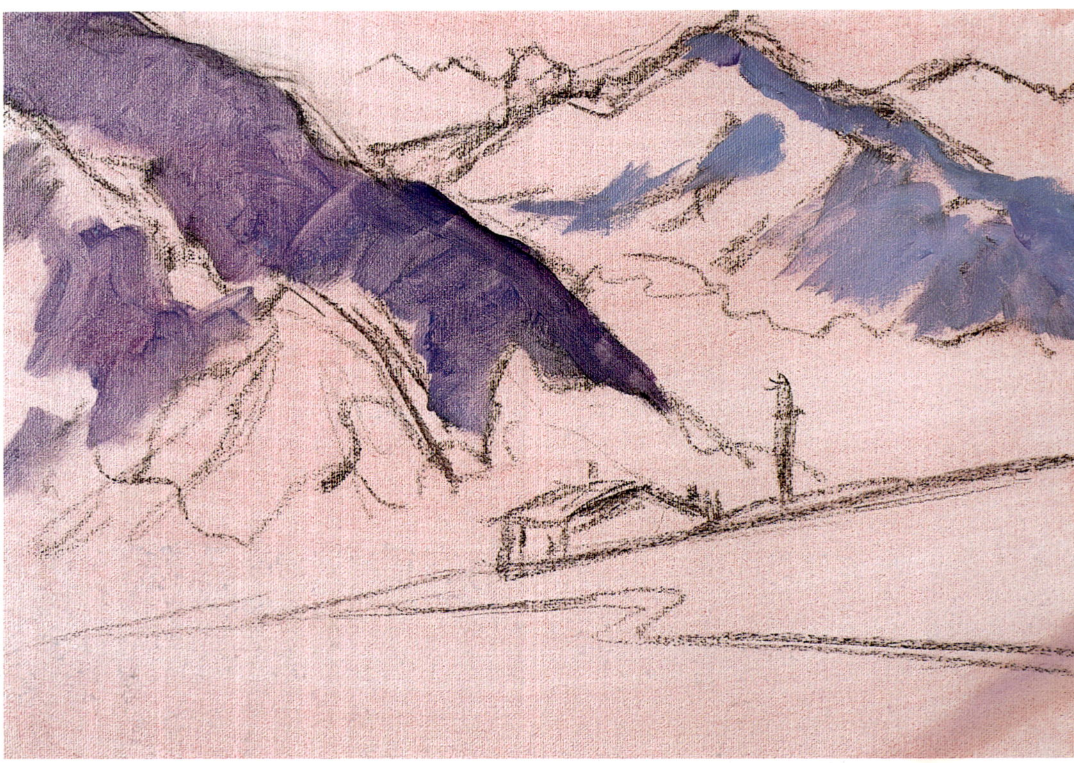

▲ First stage

Colours

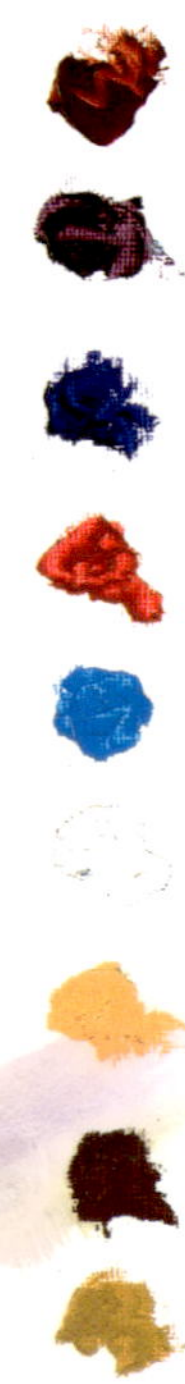

Alizarin Crimson
Cobalt Violet
French Ultramarine
Rose Madder
Coeruleum
Titanium White
Naples Yellow
Venetian Red
Yellow Ochre

First Stage

I worked on a background wash of Alizarin Crimson acrylic. This cool pink ground would help to harmonize the cool blues and greys. I started by sketching in the overall composition with charcoal. Next, I put in the darkest tones of the foreground mountain using Cobalt Violet and French Ultramarine thinned with alkyd medium to give a translucent effect. Dark tones for the right-hand mountain were paler and more opaque, so I painted these with Rose Madder, Coeruleum and white.

Second Stage

Next I put in a flat sky with Coeruleum and Titanium White. Using the flat edge of a 12 mm (½ in) brush, I painted the sharp angles of the distant peaks. Highlights to the main mountains were Naples Yellow and

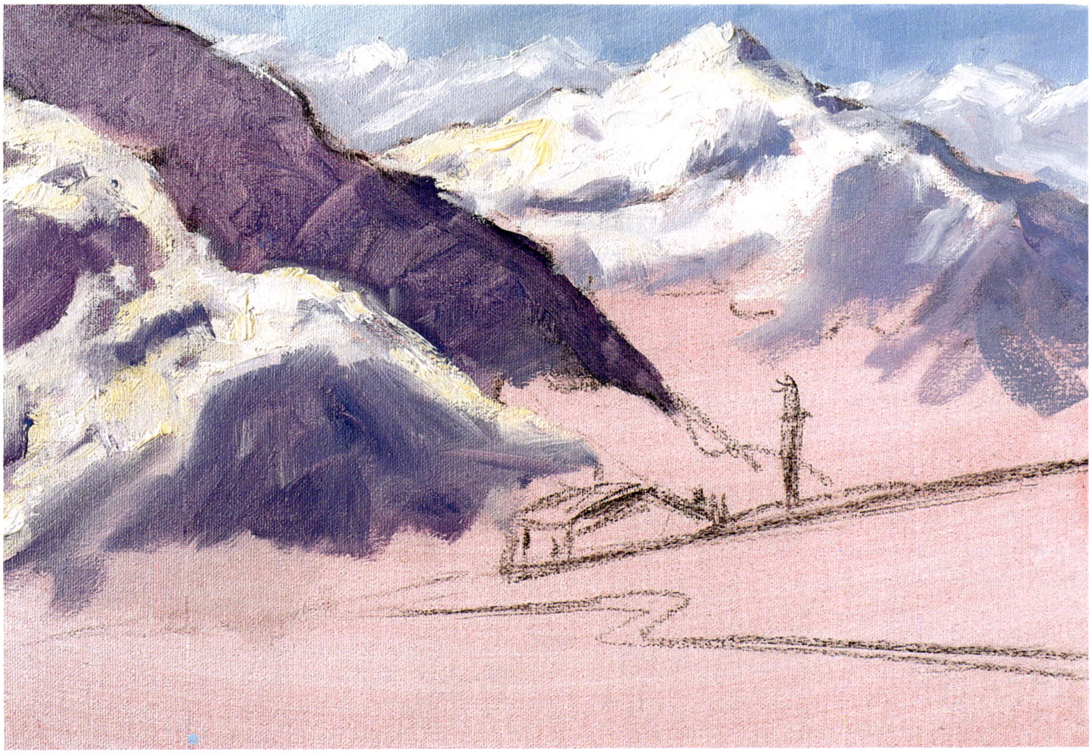

◀ Second stage

Titanium White, painted with no medium to give them a strong impact against the more thinly painted shadows.

Third Stage

The mountain hut helps to add a sense of scale as well as colour. I used Venetian Red and Cobalt Violet for the shadow side of the building, the chimney, windows and mast. Yellow Ochre and Titanium White were used for the sunlit front. The foreground snowfield was Naples Yellow and white, painted with loose sweeping brushstrokes to give a sense of the gentle slope downwards.

▶ Third stage

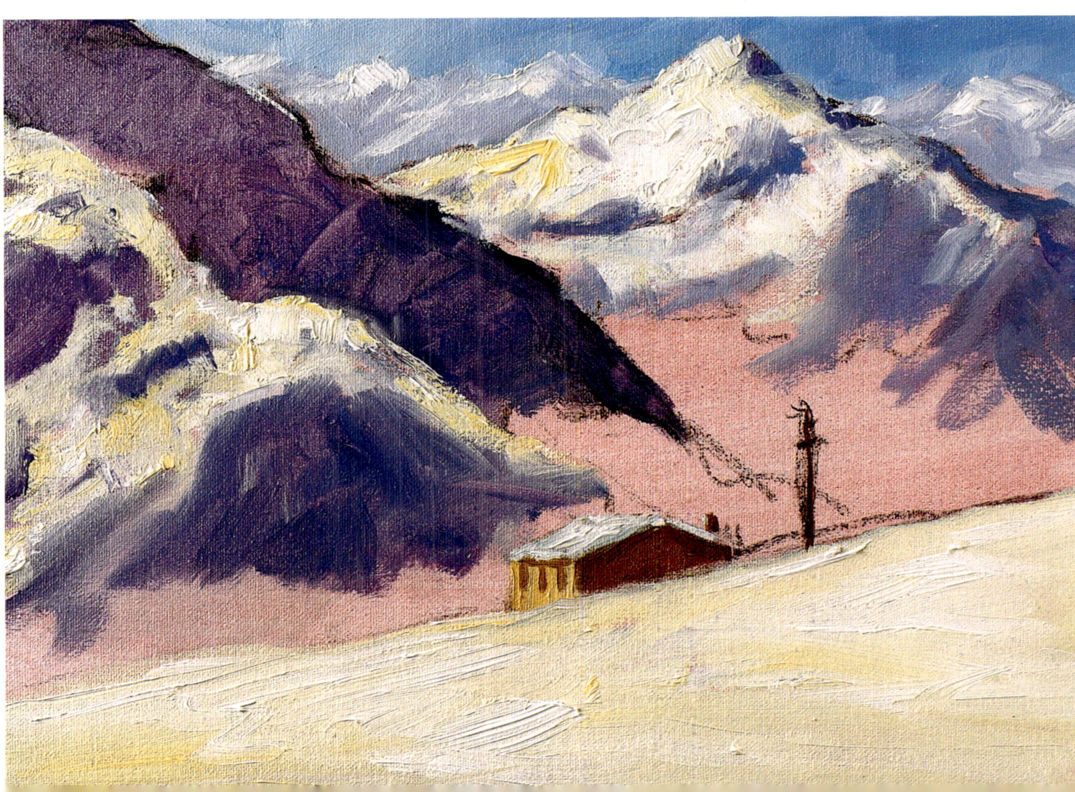

Finished Stage

To paint the mist in the bottom of the valley, I used Naples Yellow and white with plenty of alkyd medium. I put on the paint with my finger, gently rubbing and blending the paint onto the canvas, adding a little Cobalt Violet for the shadows within the mist. Finally, I used the sharp edge of the 12 mm (½ in) flat brush to mark in the ski tracks sweeping past the mountain hut.

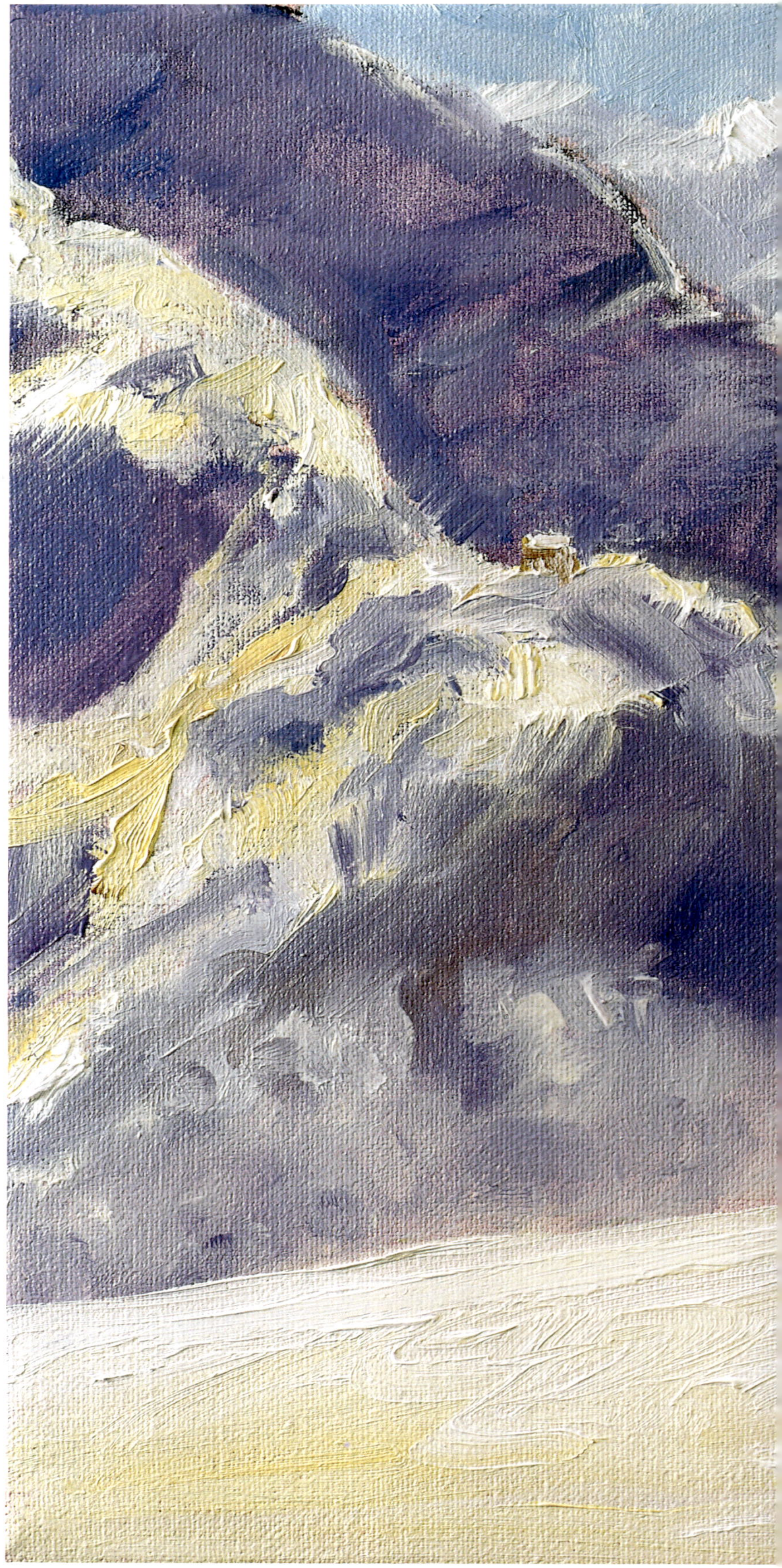

▶ **Alpine View**
10 x 14 cm (25 x 35 in)

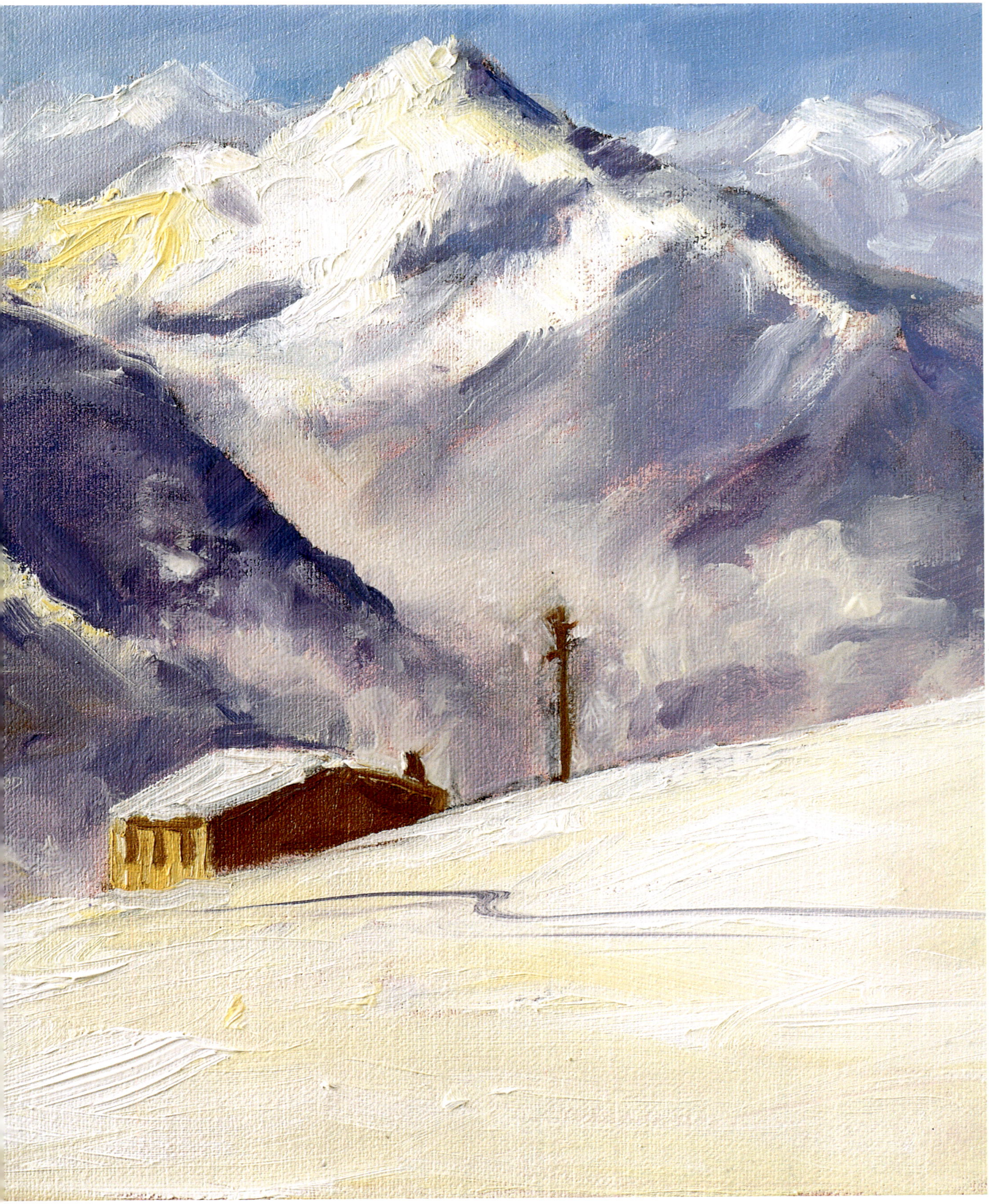

DEMONSTRATION THREE

Autumn Woodland

Woodlands can be magical places to paint, especially in autumn. I concentrated on keeping my colours soft, using violets and blues in the distance to contrast against the golds and yellows of the foreground. The vertical format helps add height. I let the foreground trees grow out of the top of the painting for the same reason.

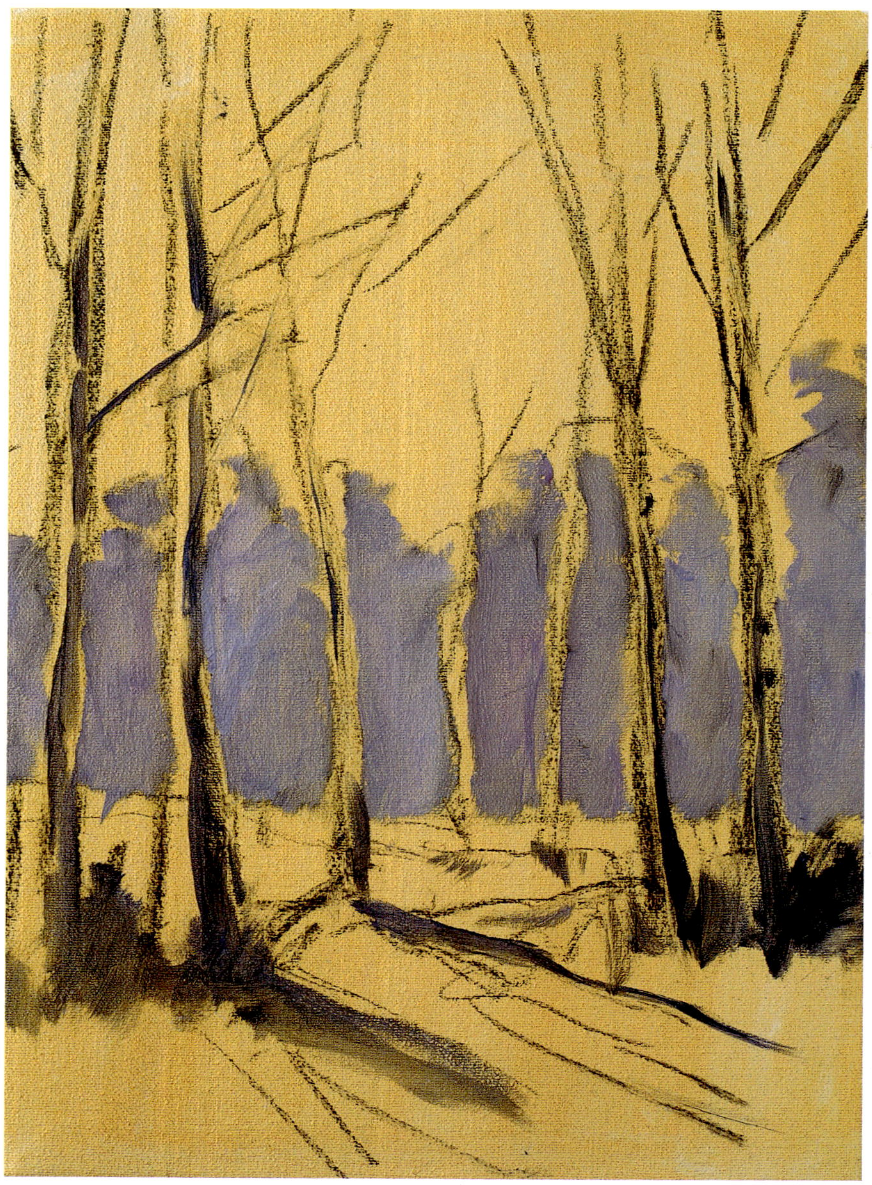

◀ First stage

Colours

- Yellow Ochre
- Cobalt Violet
- French Ultramarine
- Coeruleum
- Titanium White
- Naples Yellow
- Lemon Yellow
- Vermilion

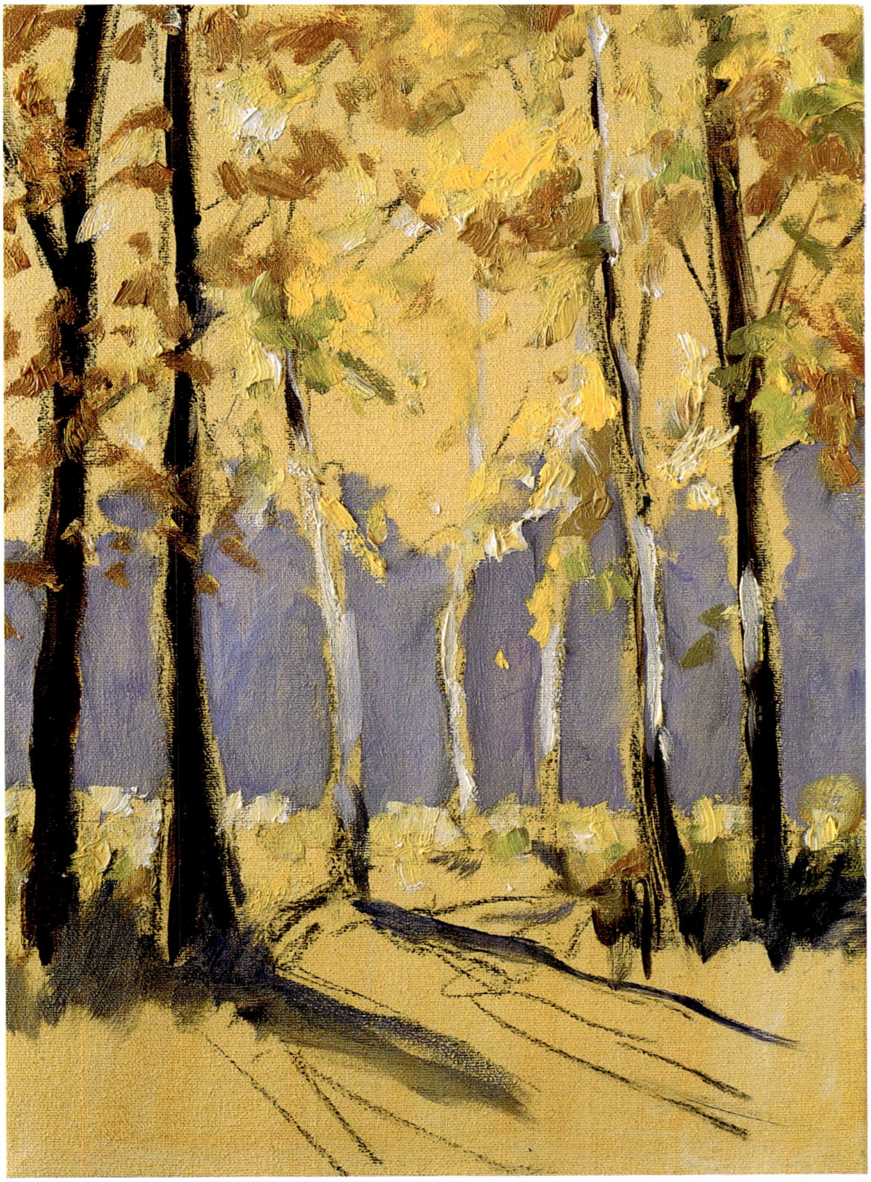

▶ Second stage

First Stage

I chose a background wash of Yellow Ochre so that any flecks of unpainted canvas would add light and colour to the finished woodland. After drawing in the main trees with charcoal, I put in the shadows on these trees with Cobalt Violet and French Ultramarine, marking in their shadows across the path at the same time. Then, using a 12 mm (½ in) brush, I blocked in the bank of distant trees with Cobalt Violet, Coeruleum and Titanium White, letting the brushstrokes go in different directions.

Second Stage

Using the 6 mm (¼ in) brush with Naples Yellow and Titanium White, I painted the trunks of the silver birch trees, before changing back to the 12 mm (½ in) brush to block in the main areas of foliage. For these I used Lemon Yellow for the sunlit leaves, Yellow Ochre and Vermilion for the warm orange patches and Lemon Yellow with Coeruleum for the few patches of bright green, working loosely to add movement and interest. Sunlit areas under the trees are Lemon Yellow and white.

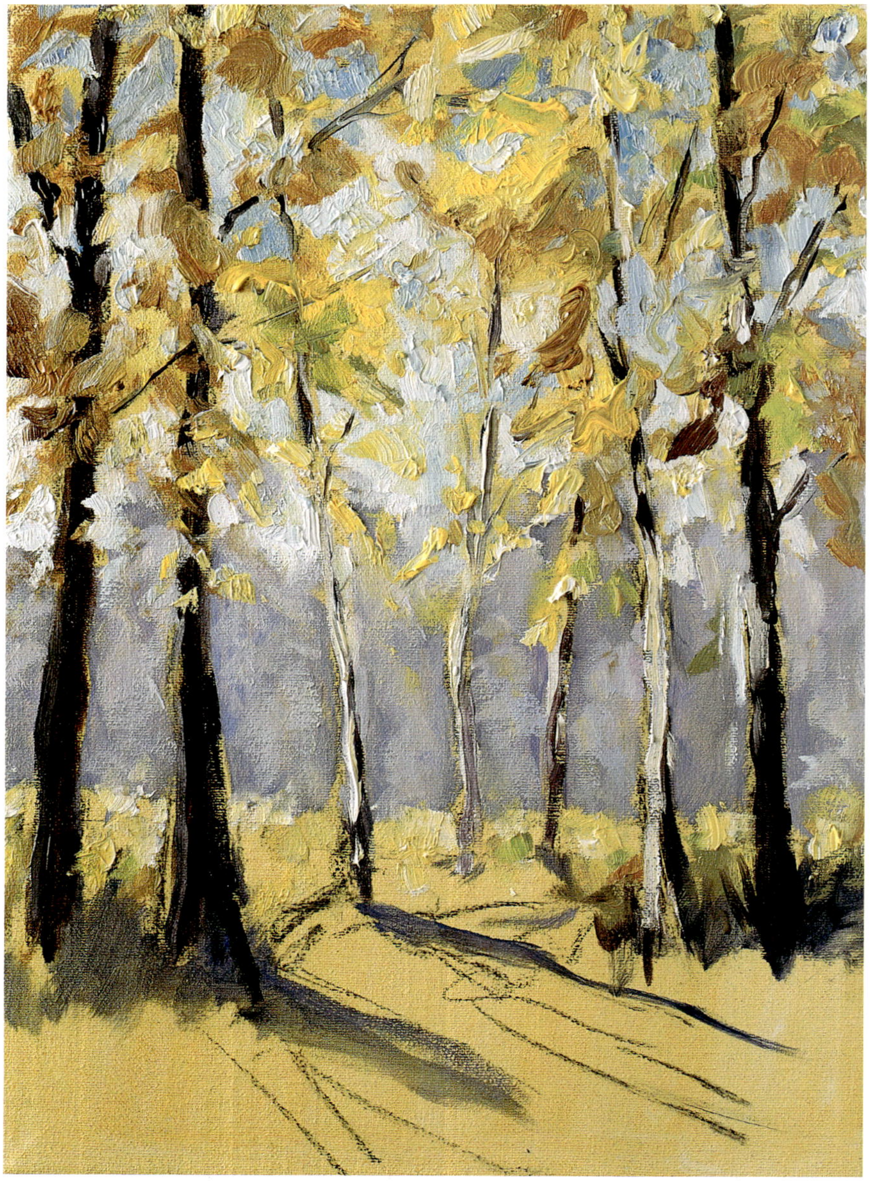

◀ Third stage

Third Stage

For the sky holes I loaded the 12 mm (½ in) brush with Coeruleum and Titanium White and gently pushed patches of blue between the already wet areas of foliage. Twigs and smaller branches were restated with the No. 4 round brush. I then stippled a softer purple tone into the background trees to help break up any large flat areas of colour.

Finished Stage

Next I painted the footpath with Naples Yellow and Titanium White, adding shadows with Cobalt Violet and Coeruleum. Foreground grasses were Yellow Ochre and Coeruleum, with Lemon Yellow for the sunlit patches. I softened the middle ground by adding a few patches of soft violet into the grasses along the edge of the footpath.

▶ **Autumn Woodland**
14 x 10 cm (35 x 25 in)

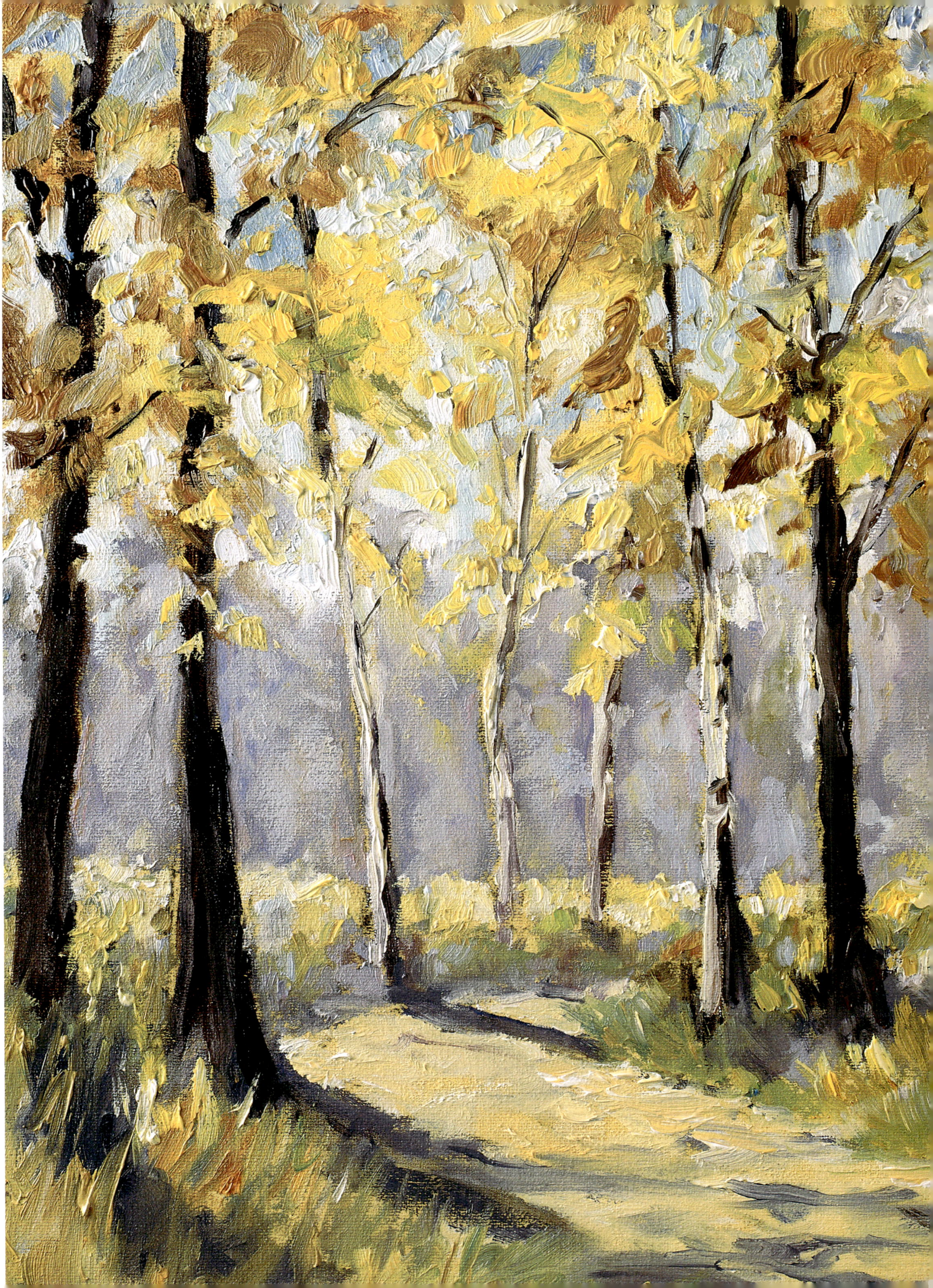

DEMONSTRATION FOUR

French Lavender

Coming across a field of lavender is an absolute delight, and an ideal subject to paint. I have kept the composition simple, letting the colours speak for themselves. To create recession in the lavender rows I painted those in the middle ground as simple stripes, adding textural detail to the foreground only with jagged brushstrokes.

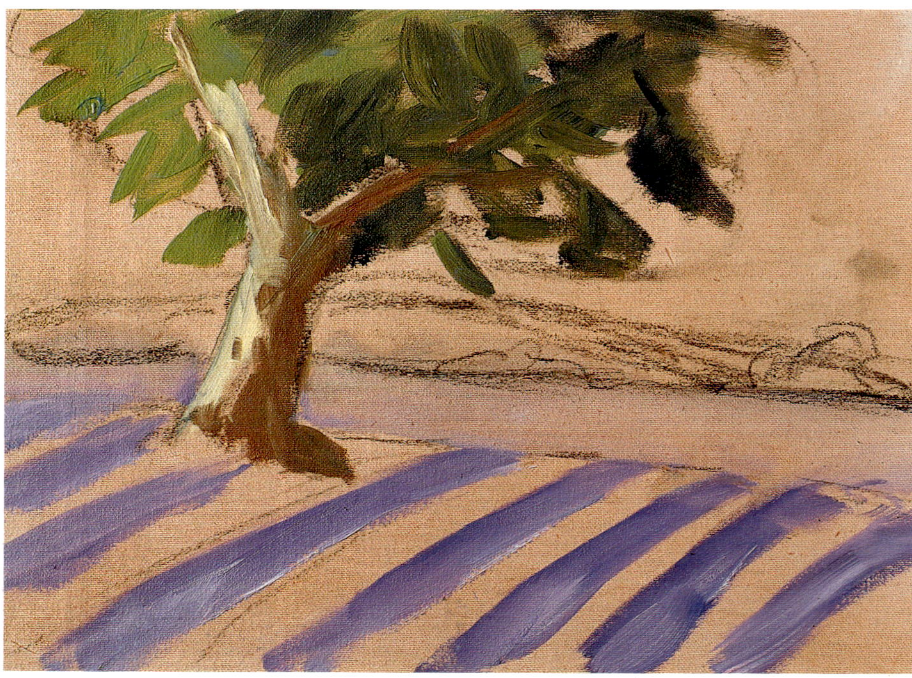

▶ First stage

Colours

- Vermilion
- Yellow Ochre
- French Ultramarine
- Coeruleum
- Venetian Red
- Naples Yellow
- Rose Madder
- Titanium White
- Cobalt Blue

First Stage

First I gave my canvas a thin wash of Vermilion. This cool pink shade provides an ideal background to both the warm lavender shades and the cooler greens of the tree and distant hillside. After sketching in the tree and background hill with charcoal, I used a 12 mm (½ in) flat brush to block in the main tree using Yellow Ochre and French Ultramarine for the dark foliage, changing to Coeruleum for the lighter green. The tree was painted using a 6 mm (¼ in) flat brush. Shadows on the trunk itself are Venetian Red, with pure Naples Yellow for the highlights. The foreground lavender was indicated with simple stripes of Rose Madder and French Ultramarine.

Second Stage

Next I put in the distant hillside, using an atmospheric pale grey-green, before painting soil stripes in the middle ground using Naples Yellow and white. Note how these lines run in the opposite direction to the foreground rows of lavender. The sky was then painted with Cobalt Blue and

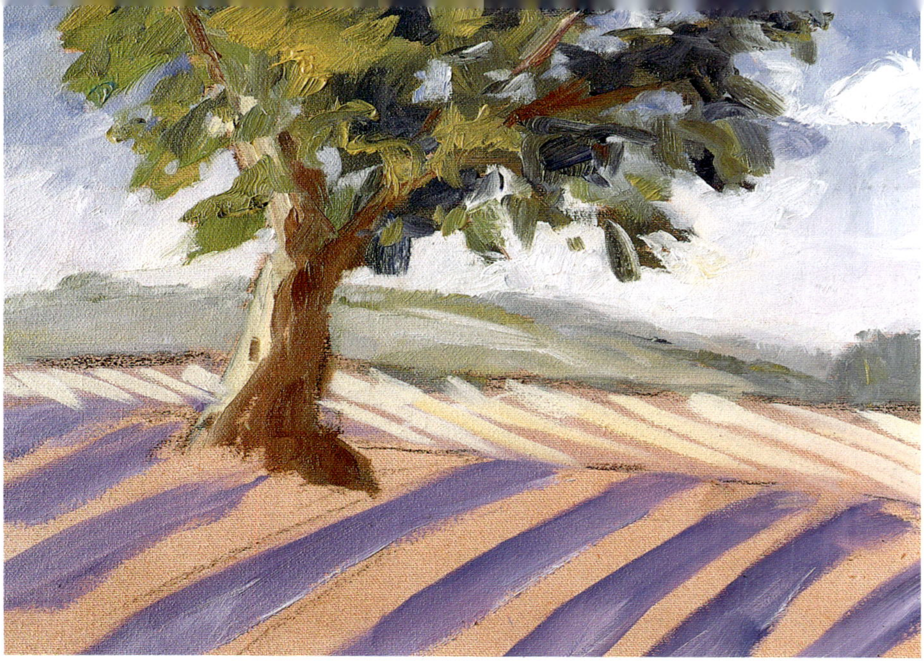

◀ Second stage

Titanium White, working a few sky holes into the tree and adding a little Rose Madder towards the horizon.

Finished Stage

I painted the middle-distance lavender as simple stripes of colour, using Rose Madder, Coeruleum and Titanium White. The lack of detail here helps to keep them visually in the distance. I put in more soil colour between the foreground rows of lavender. Then I used the edge of the 6 mm (¼ in) brush to paint the spiky texture of the foreground lavender using Rose Madder and French Ultramarine. Finally, I put in the shadow of the tree with Venetian Red. The result was a simple scene that reminded me of a wonderful day in the South of France.

▼ **French Lavender**
10 x 14 cm (25 x 35 in)

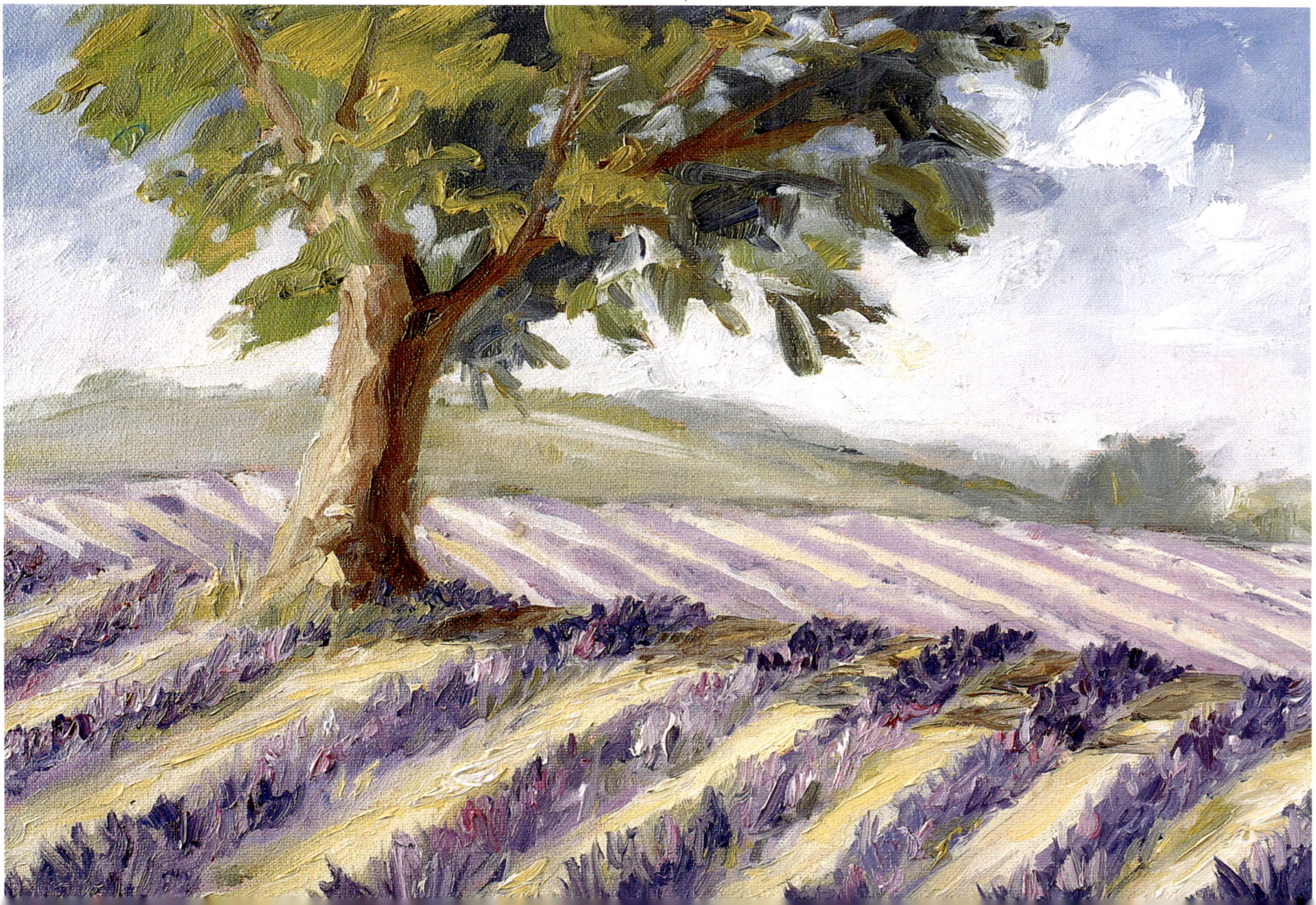

Collins

THE NEXT STEP ...

If you have enjoyed this book, why not have a look at other art instruction titles from Collins?

Other titles in the *Learn to Paint* series include:

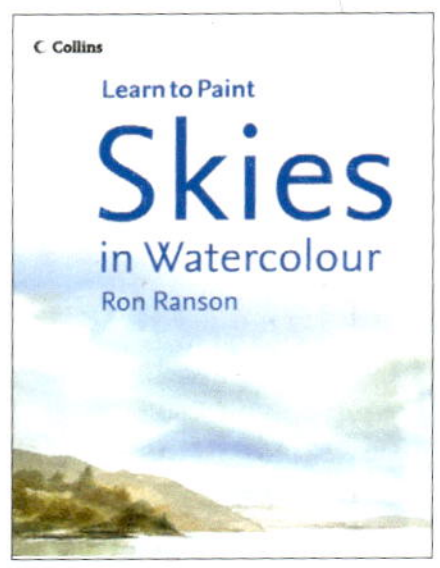

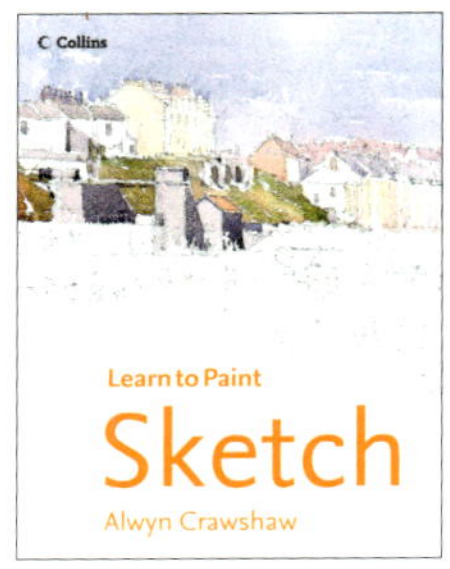

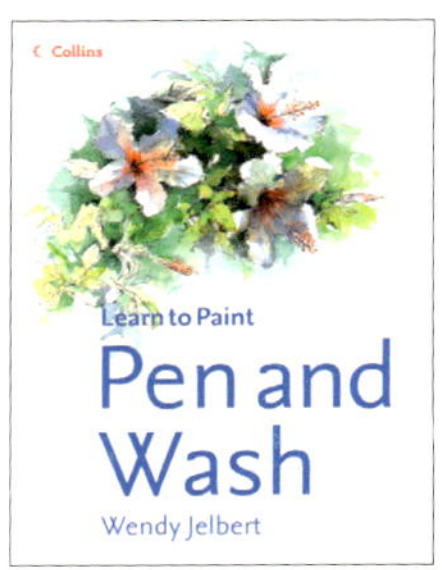

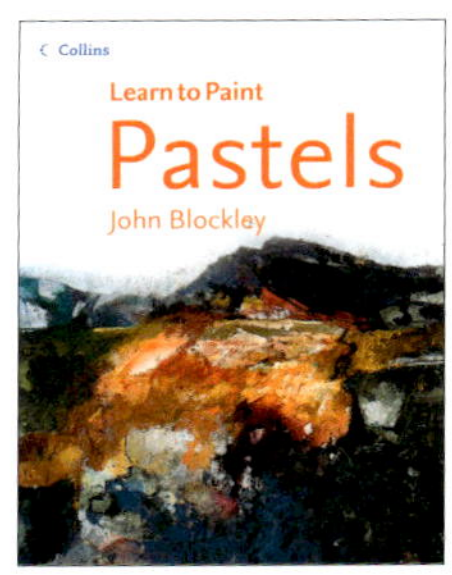

And if you want to take your painting further, try these titles:

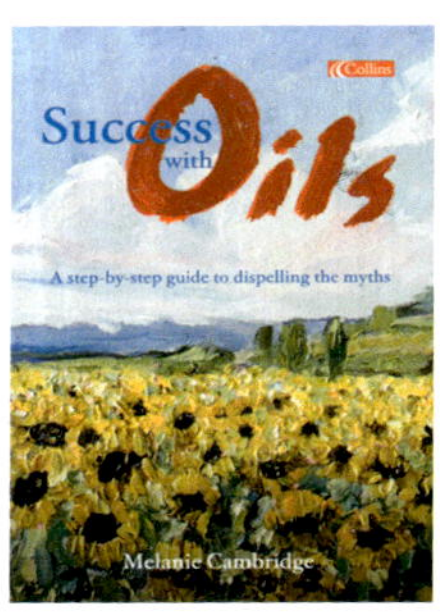

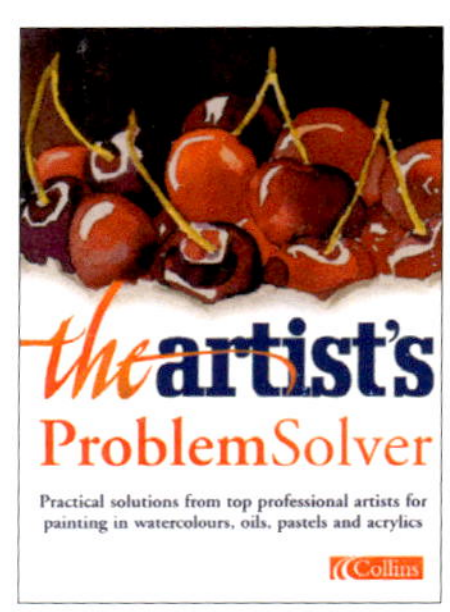

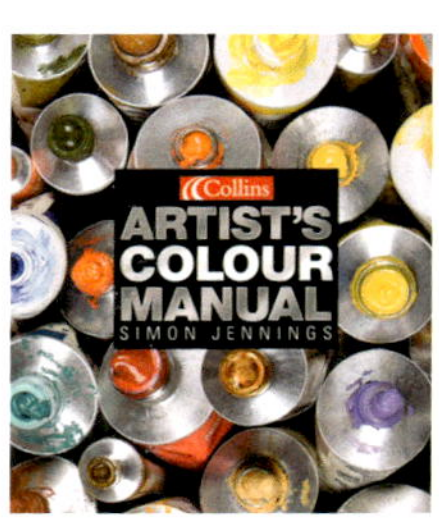

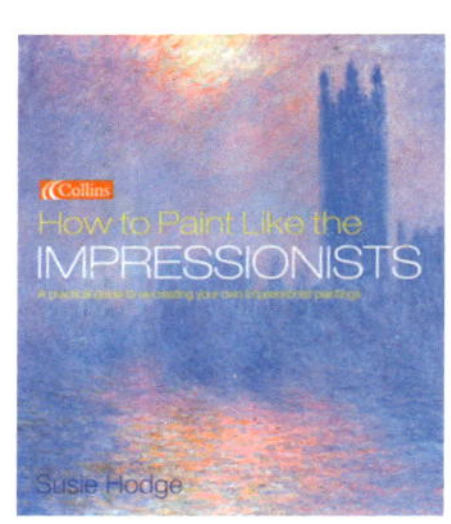

To order any of these titles, please telephone **0870 787 1732**
For further information about Collins books, visit our website: www.collins.co.uk

Some other addresses and websites you might find useful are:

ART MAGAZINES

The Artist, Caxton House, 63/65 High Street, Tenterden, Kent TN30 6BD; tel: 01580 763673
www.theartistmagazine.co.uk

Artists & Illustrators, The Fitzpatrick Building, 188-194 York Way, London N7 9QR; tel: 020 7700 8500

Leisure Painter, Caxton House, 63/65 High Street, Tenterden, Kent TN30 6BD; tel: 01580 763315
www.leisurepainter.co.uk

ART MATERIALS

Daler-Rowney Ltd, Bracknell, Berkshire RG12 8ST; tel: 01344 424621
www.daler-rowney.com

Winsor & Newton, Whitefriars Avenue, Wealdstone, Harrow, Middlesex HA3 5RH; tel: 020 8427 4343
www.winsornewton.com

ART SOCIETIES

Society for All Artists (SAA), P. O. Box 50, Newark, Nottinghamshire NG23 5GY; tel: 01949 844050
www.saa.co.uk

BOOKCLUBS

Artists' Choice, P. O. Box 3, Huntingdon, Cambridgeshire PE28 0QX; tel: 01832 710201
www.artists-choice.co.uk

INTERNET RESOURCES

Art Museum Network: the official website of the world's leading art museums
www.amn.org

Artcourses: an easy way to find part-time classes, workshops and painting holidays
www.artcourses.co.uk

Painters Online: interactive art club run by The Artist's Publishing Company
www.painters-online.com

VIDEOS

APV Films, 6 Alexandra Square, Chipping Norton, Oxfordshire OX7 5HL; tel: 01608 641798
www.apvfilms.com

Teaching Art, P. O. Box 50, Newark, Nottinghamshire NG23 5GY; tel: 01949 844050
www.teachingart.com